Understanding Audio and Video
by Michael Riggs

Acknowledgments

Many thanks to Michael Riggs for a very fine piece of writing; to Mike Fidler and Steve Schein at Pioneer for their help in editing; and to Bill Tynan for going the distance.

Credits

Design and Production by Robin L. Strelow
Technical Illustrations by Alice Topf
Cover Illustration by Robert Pizzo

Preface

In 1971, Pioneer first published a book called *Understanding High Fidelity*. It was written for consumers but ended up in the back pockets of most of the country's retail audio salespeople as an industry reference. The book's popularity warranted nine reprintings.

In its last revision in 1977, the book explained the hot, new technologies of the day, such as a "pulse-noise suppressor circuit" in tuners. That year, the turntable was the most common source of prerecorded music in American homes. And the marriage of audio and video was years off; the two had not yet been formally introduced.

Times, and technologies, have changed, and, as a company responsible for many of those changes, Pioneer has once again published a guide to home entertainment, revising the title to reflect the current popularity of video products. We asked *Stereo Review,* another long-time industry authority, and Michael Riggs, the magazine's editor at large, to join us in presenting the book. We hope you find it enlightening. And for some of you, we hope that it changes your outlook on these products somewhat, from little, black boxes of technology to tools that you can use to enhance and shape your lifestyle.

Mark Smith
Pioneer Electronics
October 1989

Contents

Introduction

Modern technology has made it pretty easy to go out and buy a decent television set or an okay stereo system. But if you were the sort of person who could be satisfied with just "okay," you probably wouldn't even have picked up this book. There's a big difference between the best and the ordinary in audio and video equipment—a difference you can see, hear, and sometimes even feel.

However, as the pace of innovation has quickened and the variety of products has mushroomed, buying an audio-video system has become increasingly complex. You may feel that you have wandered into a tangled maze of unfamiliar features, cryptic buzzwords, conflicting claims, and inscrutable specifications. Fortunately, a little knowledge can be a powerful tool. The purpose of this book is to help you make sense of the choices before you—to make you a smart shopper who goes home at the end of the day confident and happy rather than confused and frustrated.

The first thing to understand is that getting something better doesn't necessarily mean spending a lot more money. On the other hand, a little extra investment often is worth the result. (After all, you can play music on a table radio, but it's a very different experience.) And it's always a good idea to buy with the future in mind, especially if you are working on a tight budget. Often the best strategy is to get as good a core system as you can—one that handles all the basic audio and video functions you want to have immediately, for example—and then add on to it gradually as finances permit. This helps ensure that the system you wind up with is one that will satisfy your needs for many years to come.

The Marriage of Audio and Video

One key reason for taking a careful step-by-step approach when your budget is limited is the growing integration of audio and video: wide-range stereo (and now digital) soundtracks on laser videodiscs*; hi-fi sound on VCRs; stereo television broadcasts; music videos; CD Videos (CD-Vs); combination CD/CD-V/LD players that handle the whole gamut of advanced, high-performance audio- and videodisc formats; and home surround-sound processors. These exciting developments, together with high-resolution video monitors and multipurpose pro-

*To avoid confusion, we will refer to all 8- and 12-inch optically read videodiscs as *laser videodiscs*. (There have been other types of videodiscs, but the laser-read variety is the only one now available in the United States.) Elsewhere, you may sometimes see these discs called CD Videos or CD-Vs. We will reserve those terms for 5-inch discs containing approximately 20 minutes of music (in standard Compact Disc format) plus a short music video with a digital soundtrack.

grammable remote controls, have created a strong incentive to merge your equipment into a unified audio-video system that can do full justice to both picture and sound, no matter how they are packaged. We will be examining the questions raised by audio-video integration throughout the book.

The Quest for High Fidelity

The goal of all this ever-advancing technology is high fidelity: the most accurate and realistic reproduction of the original sound or image. It is a tantalizing and elusive goal. And though we are much closer to it than we were 40 years ago, when the idea of high-fidelity audio first began to take hold, we probably will never quite arrive. It is not reasonable to expect a perfect replica of a concert in your living room, for example. But from a good recording, you should get a plausible rendition—perhaps even one that lets you forget from time to time that you really haven't left your home.

Among the most important judgments you will have to make of an audio or video component before buying is how well it serves the cause of high fidelity. To that end, we will be discussing which factors affect audible and visible performance (and which don't), how to interpret the important specifications, and how to look and listen critically.

Although some of the explanations in the book are necessarily a little technical, we have tried to convey the essential information without getting bogged down in unnecessary detail (and with liberal use of charts and diagrams wherever they can help clarify). And there is a glossary to help you through the terminology. We think the operation of audio and video equipment is fascinating and that figuring out what to buy can be fun. We hope, by the end, you feel at least a little bit the same way.

Chapter 1

Audio and
Audio-Video Systems

Audio and
Audio-Video Systems

What you hear when you listen to music on a stereo system—or even on something as simple as a table radio—is the last step in a long process that usually begins in a recording studio (although recordings sometimes are made on location at concert halls or other sites). There, musicians play into microphones. A microphone works like a loudspeaker in reverse. It contains a small diaphragm that vibrates in sympathy with the sound waves from the instruments and converts these vibrations into tiny electrical currents, which are then amplified and fed through a recording console to a tape recorder. The recordings created in the studio become the raw material from which a Compact Disc, cassette, or phonograph record is made.

The Playback System

Although the recording and production stages of getting music from the studio or concert hall to your home are of crucial importance to the quality of what you finally hear, they are out of your control. What you can do, however, is make sure that whatever winds up on disc or tape is reproduced as accurately and pleasingly as possible in your home. The choices you make when you assemble your audio system will determine how close you come to the ideal of perfect reproduction—and how satisfied you are with what you hear.

An audio system reverses the recording process, taking the signals recorded on a disc or tape and converting them back into sound. Even in an all-in-one tape or record player, this involves a number of discrete steps that are mirrored in the layout of a component audio system. Such a system starts with components designed to read the information from the storage or transmission medium: Compact Disc player, tape deck, FM tuner, and turntable. In North America, the tuner usually is combined with a preamplifier and power amplifier in a single unit called a *receiver,* but treating them as separate pieces will help clarify the underlying structure of an audio system.

These signal sources feed a preamplifier, which has two basic functions. Its first job is to bring all of the signals coming into it up to a level suitable for driving a power amplifier. The other, more obvious task it performs is that of control. It is on the preamp that you will find source selectors, volume and tone controls, and so forth. And any self-respecting preamplifier will provide one or more sets of jacks for tape recorders or signal processors (equalizers and the like) so that you

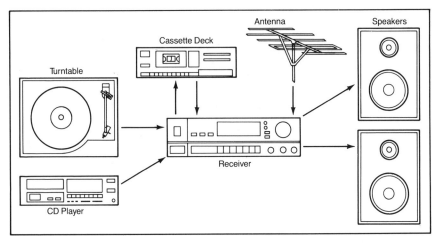

A Typical Audio System

can make your own recordings from discs or off the air.

Normally, the main output from the preamplifier goes directly to a power amplifier, which gives the system its muscle. A power amp's only job is to make the signal strong enough to drive a loudspeaker to the volume level you want when you listen to your music. Although this function appears simple, the bare description is deceptive. We will have a great deal more to say about power amplifiers in the next chapter, on receivers.

At the end of this long chain is a loudspeaker. Like a microphone, a loudspeaker is a type of transducer: a device designed to convert one form of energy into another. It transforms the electrical output from the power amp into mechanical motion of one or more diaphragms (usually cones or domes made of paper, plastic, or even metal). The vibration of these diaphragms creates sound waves similar to those originally picked up by the microphones in the recording studio. Unfortunately, creating an exact replica is very difficult, and even the best speakers alter the signals fed to them far more than any other audio component. Consequently, the loudspeakers you choose will have the greatest overall effect on the sound of your audio system.

From Mono to Stereo

Those are the basics of any audio system, no matter how simple. But nowadays it is taken for granted that a system designed for high-fidelity reproduction will also deliver stereophonic sound, or *stereo*. Although nearly everyone knows that stereo requires the use of two loudspeakers, it is clear from the way these speakers often are installed that many people don't understand why they have more than one. A mono-

ᴐ. Monophonic re-
ɲg cannot correctly
ᵖᵥ ʳay the relative loca-
tions of sound sources.

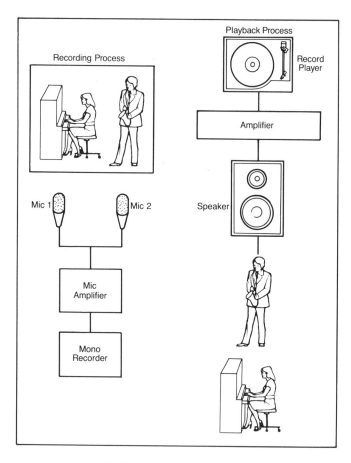

phonic system, which carries all the audio information on a single channel, can be very good in all respects except one: All the sound comes from a single point. The result is a closed, constricted sonic image that conveys no sense of the spatial relationships among the instruments on a recording.

Stereo largely overcomes this deficiency, providing an excellent rendition of where instruments are located from left to right across the stage and even, in good recordings, a fair sense of their placement front-to-back (depth) and of the acoustic space in which the recording was made. (Surround-sound can deliver an even better approximation of true three-dimensional reproduction, especially with Dolby Surround–encoded movies, but that's a story for later.) Although the first commercial stereo records were made in the 1950s, the theory behind the process was well-established before the start of World War II. It works by tricking the mechanisms the human auditory system uses to determine which direction a sound is coming from.

We use two main types of cues to localize a sound. One is the dif-

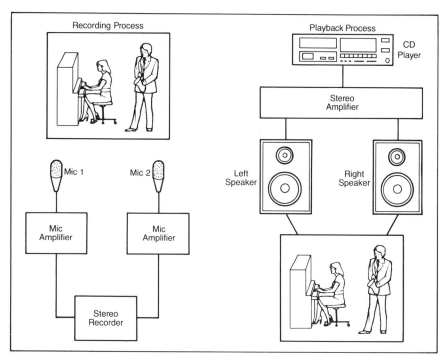

Stereo. Stereophonic recording and playback preserve the spatial relationships between instruments.

ference between the times at which a sound arrives at our two ears. A sound originating from your right will reach your right ear slightly before the left, and vice versa. The greater the difference, the greater the angle away from straight ahead at which the source is located. The other major indicator is difference in intensity at the two ears. We perceive sounds as being more in the direction of the ear in which they are louder, with, again, the angle being proportional to the difference.

Stereo uses two audio channels to mimic these cues in such a way that we hear sounds as emanating from various locations between a pair of spaced loudspeakers, even though they actually are coming from the speakers themselves. For example, let's imagine that you are sitting in front of and midway between a pair of stereo loudspeakers. If a singer's voice is played through the speakers so that it emerges from both at the same time and the same level, you will perceive it as coming from a single position directly in front of you. If it is played through only one of the speakers, it will sound as though it is coming from that direction. And if it is played at a slightly higher level through one speaker than the other, the singer will appear to be located somewhere between the midpoint and the louder speaker. This is called the *stereo effect,* and the illusory staging of the musicians is called *stereo imaging.*

Although you can play a stereo recording monophonically (by mixing the two channels of information that normally would be routed to separate speakers into a single channel), true stereo effect cannot be obtained from a mono recording. The simplest way to make a stereo recording is to set up a pair of microphones in front of the musicians and send the outputs from the mikes to separate tracks on a tape recorder. If those two channels of information are kept separate all the way to your loudspeakers, and you have the speakers properly set up in front of and approximately equidistant from your listening position, you will get stereo sound. In practice, stereo recording is seldom quite that easy, but the idea remains the same even when the technique is slightly different.

The basic stereo image created by a recording is determined before you get your hands on it. What you do with it does make an important difference, however. The type of loudspeakers, where they are placed, whether or not you use any sort of surround-sound processing, and the acoustics of your listening room all affect the quality of the stereo image you hear. These are matters we will take up in more detail later.

Stereo Image. In stereo, the apparent position of a sound is determined by the relative strengths of its signal in the two channels. For example, if its signal is equally strong in both channels, the sound will appear to be centered between the speakers.

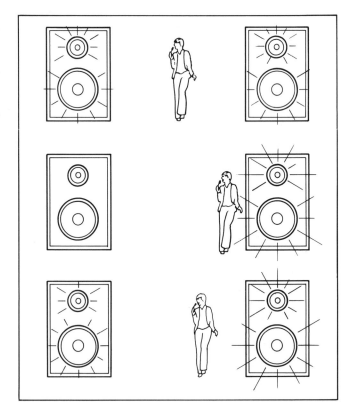

Compacts, Rack Systems, and Components

There are several approaches to buying an audio system. One is to buy a compact, all-in-one unit that combines most of the essential functions onto a single chassis. Although compact systems typically are easy to use and relatively inexpensive, they can be weak on performance and often are difficult to expand.

A more elaborate type of prepackaged system consists of separate components (receiver, tape deck, CD player, and so forth) from a single manufacturer in a piece of furniture designed to hold them. These one-brand rack systems are easy to buy and use and can deliver good sound, but you may have trouble finding one that exactly suits your requirements.

If performance, flexibility, and a perfect fit to your lifestyle are your overriding concerns, the best option is to shop for individual components that can be assembled into a complete system tailored specifically to your needs and tastes. This requires more thought and effort on your part, but a good dealer and some time spent reading this book and the various audio magazines will help you on your way.

Stepping Up to Audio-Video

Among the most exciting developments in audio over the last decade has been its deepening relationship with video. A television set used to be the equivalent of a table radio with a picture tube, and that's about all people expected of it. But as VCRs, videodiscs, projection television, and high-performance monitor/receivers came on the market, that perception began to change. Then came Dolby Stereo in movie theaters and its domestic counterpart, Dolby Surround, hi-fi sound on VCRs, and CD-quality digital sound on laser videodiscs.

TV still serves the role of radio with pictures, but now it increasingly is the central element in a home screening room where you can watch feature films, concerts, and other forms of entertainment without ever straying too far from the phone, the refrigerator, or whatever else you might find it inconvenient to be away from. Even broadcast television has responded, with stereo sound on many programs and a couple of experiments in Dolby Surround.

An important consequence of this change is the emergence of integrated audio-video systems designed to handle everything from talk shows to movies to music videos to straight music (no picture). And with those systems have come components designed to bridge the gap between what used to be entirely separate entertainment systems. Even if you don't want to commit immediately to a full-blown A/V system, you should consider making your stereo system easily expandable in that direction. This involves decisions about whether to get an ordinary CD player or a combination CD/CD-V/LD player, whether to get a receiver with built-in switching for video components or to add the necessary switching later, whether to get a receiver with a built-in surround-sound decoder or to add that later, where in the room to place the system, and so forth.

On the other hand, if you love movies as much as you love music, you may want to mix the media as soon as possible. This might mean building the system around a projection television monitor and a CD/CD-V/LD player tied together through an audio-video receiver with complete A/V switching facilities, surround-sound decoder, and multichannel amplifier for driving all the necessary speakers. It's astonishing how close you can come to the movie-theater experience with such a setup (and it's the sound, as much as anything else, that makes the difference).

Or you may prefer to go with a separate tuner, preamp, and ampli-

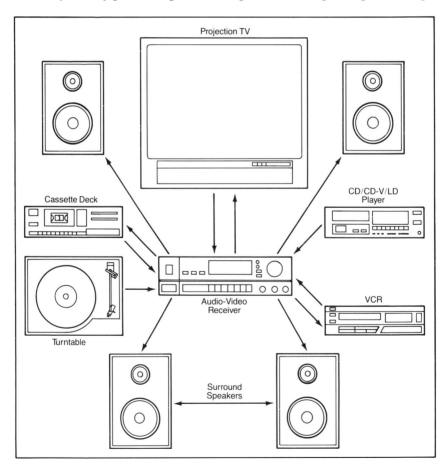

A Typical Audio-Video System

fiers and use external processors for both Dolby Surround decoding of movie soundtracks and concert-hall simulation with music recordings. We will deal with these issues in more detail in the chapters on individual components that follow.

Chapter 2

Receivers

Receivers

The nerve center of most audio systems (at least in the United States) is a *receiver*. Signals from all program sources—CD, tape, FM, and so forth—flow into it, and the ones that you choose to listen to or record flow out of it to speakers, headphones, and tape decks. What happens between input and output can be simple or complex, depending on the nature of the signal source and what you want to do with it. If you just want to listen to a Compact Disc, for example, with no signal processing at all, the receiver does little more than pick the signal off the proper input and make it big enough to drive the speakers to the volume you desire. But if you want to listen to an LP with some bass boost while copying a cassette from one tape deck to another, a bit more is involved.

Anatomy of a Receiver

The best start on figuring out what you need from a receiver is an understanding of how one is put together. A receiver comprises three basic functional elements: a tuner, a preamplifier, and a power amplifier. Essentially, a *tuner* is a radio. It picks up RF (radio frequency) signals from an antenna and converts them into audio signals. A *preamplifier* provides such basic functions as source selection; volume, balance, and tone control; mode (mono/stereo) switching; and so forth. And a *power amplifier* boosts the output signals from a preamplifier to levels great enough to make sound from a loudspeaker.

What About Separates?

If you've seen advertisements for separate preamps, power amps, and tuners, you may now be wondering why anyone would want to buy them as independent components when the functional equivalent is available in one handy bundle. The answer is similar to the reason component systems are usually so preferable to all-in-one compact systems: flexibility and performance. Buying a separate preamplifier, power amplifier, and tuner can make it easier to adapt to future technological advances (such as the recent advent of home surround-sound decoders) or to accommodate an unusual system configuration. And if you need very high power (more than 120 watts or so per channel), you're probably not going to find it in a receiver.

These are exceptional situations, however—not the rule. Few people need such large amounts of power or have setup requirements that cannot be met by a good receiver. And there is a downside to separates: cost and complexity. If you were to take apart a receiver and re-

An Audio Receiver

package it as a stack of separate components, it would have to cost more simply because of the additional boxes, panels, and power supplies required. Plus you would have to hook them all together with cables. Receivers offer the simplest, most economical approach for most people most of the time. And with modern technology, there need not be any sacrifice in performance unless, as we noted above, you want stupendous amounts of power. Consequently, we will assume receivers as the norm throughout this book.

If for some reason a receiver doesn't fit your needs, there are intermediate options short of a jump to complete separates. The most popular is a combination of preamp and power amp into what is known as an *integrated amplifier.* In Europe and Japan, where there is much less diversity of radio programming than in North America, integrated amps dominate the market. Another, less common combination is the *tuner/preamp,* which combines tuner and preamplifier on a single chassis. This is an interesting alternative that probably deserves more attention than it gets from those with a yen for high power.

What if you just like the idea of separates or can't get a certain feature you crave any other way? If you can afford it (and reasonably priced separates are available), take the plunge, by all means. Nothing wrong with having a little fun with the equipment! It's no coincidence that audio hobbyists (*audiophiles,* as they're called) almost universally prefer the last iota of flexibility and performance provided by good separates over the relative economy afforded by the sensible receiver.

How Tuners Work

As we've already noted, the function of a tuner is to receive radio broadcasts. There are two basic methods of radio transmission: AM (amplitude modulation) and FM (frequency modulation). AM is the older and simpler technique. The broadcast station transmits what is called a *carrier wave* at a fixed frequency, such as 950 kHz (kilohertz).

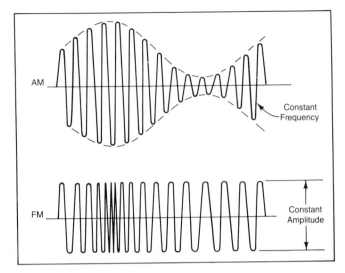

AM and FM Signals. In AM radio, the audio signal (dashed line) is represented by variations in the amplitude of a higher-frequency carrier. In FM, it is represented by variations in the frequency of the carrier, whose amplitude remains constant.

This is the frequency to which you tune a radio when you want to receive that station. The station puts audio information onto the carrier by varying the carrier's level, or *amplitude,* according to the level of the audio signal. Altering a characteristic of one waveform according to some characteristic of another is known as *modulation*—hence, in this case, amplitude modulation.

To understand fully how this works, you first need to know that all audio signals, however complicated, can be represented as a collection of smoothly varying waveforms called *sine waves.* You can imagine a sine wave as starting out from 0, rising to a maximum value,

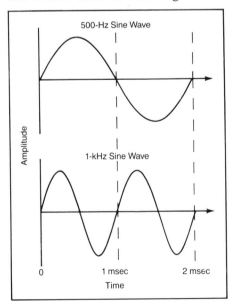

Two Sine Waves. The signal on top is exactly half the frequency (and therefore double the wavelength) of the one on the bottom. A 1-kHz sine wave completes 1,000 full cycles per second, so a single cycle takes a thousandth of a second (1 millisecond); a full cycle of a 500-Hz sine wave takes twice as long.

descending back down through 0 to a negative value equal but opposite to the maximum, and then returning to 0. That is one complete cycle of a sine wave. The number of full cycles a sine wave completes in one second is its frequency: one cycle per second (cps, in old-style terminology) is a frequency of 1 Hz (Hertz), fifty cycles per second is 50 Hz, a thousand cycles per second is 1,000 Hz (1 kHz), and so on. For a signal to be audible, its frequency must fall within the range of human hearing, which at its very best extends from approximately 20 Hz at the low end to 20 kHz at the high end.

Now, if an AM carrier is modulated with a 500-Hz tone, its level will oscillate up and down through one full cycle 500 times per second. The louder the tone, the greater the swing in the carrier's level. And if the frequency of the modulating tone is changed, the rate at which the carrier level rises and falls will change with it. (*Music* or *voice* consists of many simultaneous tones of different frequencies, which makes the waveform much more complex than that of a simple sine wave, but the principle is the same.) If you were to draw a line connecting the peaks of the much higher-frequency carrier wave, you would get a replica of the modulating audio signal. This outline is called the *envelope* of the carrier, which you might think of as riding on the carrier's back. This is how an AM radio signal conveys audio information from the transmitting station to your receiver.

An AM tuner is basically a very simple device. It first takes the signal from an antenna, which is a hodgepodge of all the carriers strong enough to be picked up, and amplifies the station frequency you have tuned in while rejecting the others around it. Then it, in effect, strips the envelope off the carrier and amplifies the resulting audio signal.

AM's chief advantages are simplicity and long transmission range. Its drawbacks are high susceptibility to noise and interference and relatively poor fidelity. Most receivers include a utilitarian AM tuner, designed mainly for low cost, high rejection of interfering signals, and good speech intelligibility. The usually correct assumption is that it will be used almost exclusively for the news and talk shows that have come to dominate AM radio as FM has taken over music programming. Although there now is a de facto standard for stereo broadcasting on the AM band, lack of such a standard in the early days of stereo AM and the relative dearth of music programming have conspired to make the necessary reception circuitry very rare in home tuners.

Frequency Modulation

The benefits and drawbacks of FM broadcasting are a mirror image of those for AM. FM requires relatively sophisticated transmitters and receivers and has much shorter range, but it also is capable of low-noise, wide-range high-fidelity sound and is far more immune to interference from things like electrical storms and power lines. An unmodulated FM carrier (that is, one with no audio signal on it) will be at the station's assigned frequency—102.5 MHz, for example. Unlike in AM, applying an audio signal does not alter the carrier's level, which remains constant. Instead, it changes the carrier's frequency.

Let's take a closer look at how this frequency modulation works. An FM transmission actually occupies a 200-kHz (0.2-MHz) channel centered on the station's nominal carrier frequency. (For example, a station's channel might be specified as 102.5 MHz, ±100 kHz.) Within that channel, FCC (Federal Communications Commission) regulations permit the carrier to deviate as much as ±75 kHz from the center frequency. So the station can actually use 150 kHz of its 200-kHz channel; the remainder is reserved for guard bands above and below the carrier, to minimize the possibility of interference with stations on nearby channels.

When modulated by an audio signal, the FM carrier frequency varies up and down around its assigned center. The louder the audio, the wider the frequency swings of the carrier, up to the ±75-kHz maximum. The frequency of the carrier follows the amplitude of the audio, which means in turn that the frequency of the audio signal is reflected in the carrier frequency's rate of change. In other words, a full-level 1-kHz tone would cause the FM carrier to go from its center frequency to +75 kHz, back to center, to −75 kHz, and then back to center again one thousand times per second; a 200-Hz tone at 40-percent modulation would shift the carrier ±30 kHz two hundred times per second; and so forth.

Stereo FM

What we've described so far is how a single channel of audio is transmitted on an FM carrier—mono. But almost every FM station in America broadcasts in stereo. This is achieved by piggybacking additional information onto the basic mono signal. In FM, the mono signal extends up to about 15 kHz. A stereo broadcast adds two additional signals: a 19-kHz pilot tone to notify receiving tuners that the transmission is stereo rather than mono and a 38-kHz subcarrier. (As its name implies, a *subcarrier* is a signal modulated onto a carrier that in turn serves as a carrier for another signal.) That subcarrier conveys what is known as a *difference signal,* which can be combined with the mono baseband signal to create separate left- and right-channel stereo signals.

A stereo broadcast starts with a stereo audio signal. The left- and right-channel signals are combined (summed) into a mono (L + R)

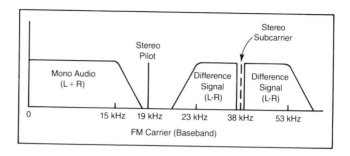

FM Signal Spectrum. The output from a tuner's FM detector consists of a mono (L + R) signal extending from approximately 30 Hz to 15 kHz, of difference-signal (L − R) information (which is later combined with the mono signal to generate stereo) amplitude-modulated onto a 38-kHz subcarrier, and of a 19-kHz pilot tone that switches on the tuner's stereo decoder.

signal that is frequency-modulated onto the main carrier. The difference signal is obtained by subtracting the right channel from the left (L − R). It is then amplitude-modulated onto the 38-kHz stereo subcarrier (which is frequency-modulated onto the main carrier). When the transmission is picked up by a stereo tuner, the tuner recognizes the 19-kHz stereo pilot tone and turns on its stereo *demodulator* (or *demultiplexer,* as it is sometimes called). This circuit takes the difference signal off the subcarrier and combines it with the mono baseband signal according to the following formulas:

$$(L + R) + (L - R) = 2L$$
$$(L + R) - (L - R) = 2R$$

And out come separate left- and right-channel signals identical to the ones we started out with back at the radio station!

FM Tuners

But we're getting a little ahead of ourselves. Before we can move on to consider features and performance specifications, we need to know a little more about how FM tuners are put together. There are five basic circuit blocks: the front end, the IF (intermediate frequency) stage, the FM detector, the stereo demodulator, and the audio output stage. An FM front end's job is to isolate the carrier you have tuned from the other carrier signals picked up by the antenna, amplify it, and convert it down to the 10.7-MHz intermediate frequency. Conversion of tuned signals to a lower, fixed frequency greatly simplifies the design of the rest of the tuner, which is relieved of having to operate over the entire 20-MHz range of the FM band.

The IF stage performs three crucial functions. One is to further amplify the still very weak signal from the front end. The second is to finish the task of paring away unwanted signals that was begun in the front end. A series of sharp, carefully adjusted filters passes signals between 10.6 and 10.8 MHz while steeply attenuating signals above and

**Block Diagram of
an FM Tuner**

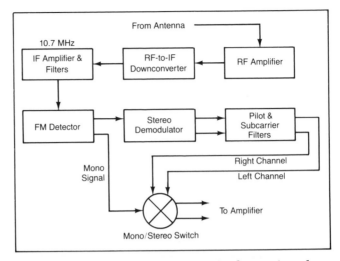

below that range. The quality of these filters largely determines how immune the tuner will be to interference between the tuned station and strong stations nearby on the dial. This very important tuner characteristic is known as *selectivity*. And finally, the IF stage includes a limiter circuit that chops the top and bottom of the carrier to remove noise picked up in transit from transmitter to receiver.

The detector is the heart of the tuner. To it falls the task of separating the audio signal from the carrier. If the signal is mono, the tuner's job is essentially done; if not, the signal must go on to the stereo demodulator. There, the difference signal is pulled off the stereo subcarrier and combined with the mono signal to derive separate left and right channels. These outputs then pass through filters designed to remove the now unwanted 19-kHz pilot tone, the 38-kHz subcarrier, and the 67-kHz SCA (Subsidiary Communication Authoriza-

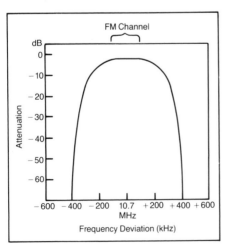

Typical IF Filter Characteristic. The filters in the intermediate-frequency (IF) stage of an FM tuner are designed to reject signals outside the tuned channel, which is downconverted to a center frequency of 10.7 MHz. Ideally, all frequencies below 10.6 MHz and above 10.8 MHz (10.7 MHz, ±100 kHz) would be sharply attenuated, but such high selectivity is difficult to achieve without significantly increased distortion of the final audio signal.

tion) signal, if one is present. (SCA is another subcarrier used by some stations to transmit background music for stores, computer data, and so forth.)

Digital vs. Analog

In the old days (that is, five or ten years ago), tuning in a station meant turning a knob to move a pointer to the correct frequency marking on a long dial. When you got close to the station, you would listen and watch a pair of meters to determine when you had it tuned dead on. One meter showed the strength of the RF signal at the antenna terminals, while the other indicated how far off the center of the channel you were tuned and in which direction. When you got the needle of the tuning meter centered, you were done—or close to it. If the markings on the dial were too close together at that point to read precisely, you might have to listen for a few minutes just to make sure you had the right station. That was *analog* tuning.

You still see some low-end tuners and receivers that work this way, but the vast majority of today's models use what is called *digital frequency synthesis* tuning. A computer on a chip (microprocessor) inside the receiver takes over the chore of tuning precisely to whatever station you want, displaying the frequency on a digital readout. This technique has all kinds of advantages, along with a couple of minor drawbacks. The main thing you lose is the ability to tune very slightly off a station's center frequency, which can reduce interference under some circumstances; most digital receivers tune in full- or half-channel steps for speed and convenience. And some people prefer the quickness and feel of a tuning knob and the precision of an analog signal-strength meter.

In fact, the latter two items are possible in a digital tuner, but are very much the exception. Manual tuning on a digital receiver normally is accomplished with up and down stepper buttons, and for cosmetic reasons the signal-strength meter usually is a row of LEDs (light-emitting diodes) that come on one after the other as the RF signal at the antenna terminal increases. Unless you have an antenna that you can rotate for best reception, a signal-strength meter is of little practical value anyway. But if you do, it can save you from having to listen to

A Separate-Component Tuner

a lot of hiss and distortion while you get the antenna properly oriented. Ideally, a signal-strength meter should be most active in the range from barely listenable to clean, quiet reception, to give you the information you need to get your antenna aimed in the right direction. So, if this is important to you, check the operation of the signal-strength meter on any receiver you are considering buying by tuning up and down the FM band and observing how the meter reading changes with sound quality.

Advantages of Digital Tuning

For most people, the benefits of digital tuning greatly outweigh its relatively minor failings (which is why you don't see many analog receivers anymore). You can push a button and have the tuner search quietly up or down (or up and down) the "dial" for the next listenable station, precisely tuning to the first one it finds. Or you can enter the frequencies of your favorite stations into the receiver's memory for instant tuning to the one of your choice at the touch of a button. And you don't have to guess to which station you've tuned from the position of a pointer on a coarsely marked dial: The frequency pops up on a digital display. There is no need for a channel-center meter, because the receiver tunes exactly to the desired station frequency.

Indeed, the opportunities for handy tuning features are almost limitless. Some receivers will store call letters when you memorize a station frequency in a preset, so that they come up on the display when you touch that button. Another possibility is direct-access tuning, by punching in the station frequency on a keypad. A really smart receiver may even let you code preset stations so that you can search through them by type (jazz, rock, classical, or whatever other categories you might find useful), listening to a little bit of each one in a group until you find just what you're looking for. And we still haven't exhausted the possibilities.

Not all of these features will interest everyone, but you may be surprised at the variety of tricks built into today's receivers and at how addictive the ones that strike your fancy can be, particularly if you listen to the radio a lot or live in an area with a large number of good stations. When shopping for a receiver, make sure you find out everything the models you're considering can do and get a demonstration of their tuning capabilities. It can make a real difference in how much enjoyment you derive from the receiver you finally buy.

Coping with Poor Reception

Another important consideration is how well the receiver handles less-than-ideal reception—weak FM signals from distant stations or sig-

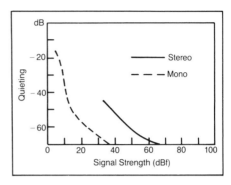

Typical FM Quieting Curves. Signal-to-noise ratio (S/N), shown on the vertical axis, improves as signal strength increases, until maximum quieting is achieved. Note that a much stronger signal is necessary for quiet stereo reception than is needed for equally quiet mono.

nals that must compete with others for your receiver's attention. Even extremely strong signals can be a source of difficulty, since they can overload the circuits in the tuner's first RF stage. This can cause the offending station to be received at multiple places on the dial, possibly blanking out or interfering with weaker stations that legitimately occupy those channels.

Front-end overload is relatively uncommon in modern tuners, however. You are far more likely to confront the opposite situation: a signal too weak for quiet reception. Every tuner exhibits a quieting curve, which is one way of representing its sensitivity to incoming signals. As RF signal strength increases, noise in the audio output goes down, until "full limiting" is reached—the point at which further increases in signal strength gain you nothing more in quieting.

An interesting thing about tuner sensitivity is how much better it is in mono than in stereo. It normally requires at least ten times the signal strength to achieve full quieting in stereo as it does in mono. So, good stereo reception is harder to achieve than clean, quiet mono. Unfortunately, this discrepancy is inherent in the stereo FM system. One characteristic of frequency modulation is that noise increases with frequency. As we noted earlier, the difference-signal information required to derive stereo is on a subcarrier at 38 kHz, well above the 15-kHz upper limit of the basic mono FM signal. Consequently, it is much noisier than the mono component, which means that the final stereo output is noisier as well. This is true even at full limiting,

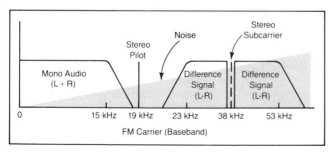

The Stereo Noise Penalty. The noise content of an FM signal increases with frequency. Because the difference-signal information used to generate stereo is carried at much higher frequencies than is the mono information, it is substantially noisier. As a result, mono reception is inherently quieter than stereo.

though, by then, both mono and stereo are quiet enough that the difference doesn't much matter. It is on signals too weak to approach full limiting in stereo that the difference is significant.

Stereo Blend

Every component receiver made today will switch automatically from stereo to mono below a certain signal strength (its stereo threshold) to prevent intolerably noisy reception, and if signal strength drops so low that even mono sounds bad, it will mute. (Most receivers will permit you to defeat the muting circuit in case you want to listen to a distant station through the noise.) There are some more sophisticated options, however, all based on moving from full stereo to mono gradually instead of all at once. In this way, it often is possible to gain an adequate degree of noise suppression without entirely losing stereo effect.

The most basic version of this feature is a simple blend switch that introduces a moderate amount of mixing between the two channels at high frequencies, where noise is the biggest problem and loss of separation between the channels is least noticeable. A better approach is for the tuner to vary the blend smoothly and automatically from a small amount strictly at high frequencies to a large amount across the board and finally to complete mono, based on the signal strength. Some FM noise-reduction systems even take into account the modulation level of the signal, since loud sounds (corresponding to a high modulation level) will mask noise better than soft sounds (low modulation) and therefore require less blend. These automatic variable-blend systems can do wonders for signals that are just a little too weak to provide good sound in full stereo.

Multipath

In a city, however, or in a hilly or mountainous region, weak-signal reception seldom is the number-one problem. The major gremlin is instead likely to be multipath: a condition in which your tuner picks up the same signal more than once, with the arrivals slightly separated in time. The later-arriving signals are reflections of the original, bounced off of buildings, hills, water towers, or other features of the local terrain—possibly even an airplane flying overhead. Unless your receiver can lock onto (capture) just one of these competing signals and suppress the others, the result will be noise and distortion. In some cases, the delays between the signals may be such that they partially cancel each other, which can further complicate matters by reducing signal strength.

The effects of multipath are worse in stereo than in mono, so the blend features mentioned above can sometimes help mitigate them.

Multipath. One of the most difficult FM-reception problems is multipath-induced distortion. Multi-path reception occurs when reflections cause a broadcast signal to reach an antenna by more than one route. Because these multiple paths have different lengths, the signals will arrive at slightly different times, which can result in cancellations and other undesirable effects.

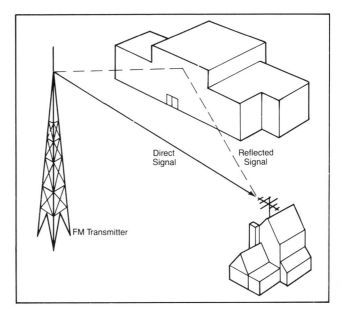

Direct Signal

Reflected Signal

FM Transmitter

Otherwise, the important things to look for in a tuner that will be used in a high-multipath environment are a low capture ratio and a high AM-suppression figure.

Selectable IF Bandwidth

As we mentioned earlier, receivers must be designed to reject signals on FM channels other than the one to which you have tuned. This is achieved with filters in the IF section of the tuner. Because extremely sharp IF filters are difficult to build and tend to produce relatively high distortion, the FCC has arranged the geographical allocation of FM channels so that stations in a particular locality are never right next door to each other on the dial: There is always at least one empty channel between them. Consequently, interference between stations on different channels is uncommon.

However, if you have a high-gain directional antenna or you live right between two large metropolitan areas, you may find that you can sometimes pick up stations on adjacent channels. Usually, the receiver will react as though it were getting two signals on the same channel and suppress the weaker one. But if one of the stations is much nearer than the other, its signal may be stronger on both channels unless the IF filters are extraordinarily steep. The result may be that the weaker station effectively disappears from your dial.

Most receivers use a compromise set of IF filters that is better than average at screening out broadcasts close in frequency to the one tuned but not good enough to sort out the kind of adjacent-channel interference described above. One solution is to provide switchable IF bandwidth. In the wide mode, minimal filtering is applied for lowest distortion when there are no interfering stations. The narrow mode, on the other hand, provides unusually sharp filtering specifically for use in situations where interference from adjacent channels is a problem.

A Word About Antennas

Although the performance of your receiver's tuner section makes a big difference to the quality of reception you get, your FM antenna is at least as important. A highly directional, rotatable antenna can be oriented to eliminate many interference problems and may prove especially useful in controlling multipath. And if you live in a fringe reception area, a high-gain outdoor antenna (preferably on a tall mast) can boost signal strength to levels adequate for clear reception of many stations that might otherwise be unacceptably noisy or lost altogether. If you are limited to using a simple omnidirectional or folded dipole indoor antenna, you may find that reception varies dramatically (both in general and from station to station) depending on where it's placed and how it's oriented. Experiment.

The Amplifier Section

As we mentioned at the beginning of the chapter, a receiver comprises three basic functional blocks: a tuner, a preamplifier, and a power amplifier. The pre- and power amplifiers often are spoken of collectively as simply the *amplifier section.* Together, they perform a number of important tasks, including selection and routing of program sources, controlling basic functions, and driving the system's loudspeakers. Since the last of these jobs is so important and accounts for such a large part of a receiver's size, weight, and cost, let's begin there.

An Integrated Amplifier

Block Diagram of a Power Amplifier

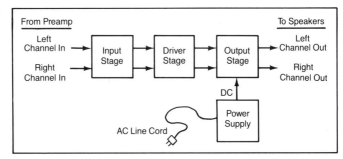

Reduced to its essentials, a power amplifier has three sections. The heftiest is the power supply, which takes alternating current (AC) from the wall, transforms it into direct current (DC), and stores it in large reservoir capacitors. But most of the parts are in the amplifying electronics—the input and driver stages—which increase the voltage of the input signal by some factor (called the *gain of the amplifier*). The business end is a set of output transistors that do the heavy work of transferring power from the amplifier to the speakers.

The output transistors operate like a set of electronic valves between the power supply and the loudspeakers, opened and closed by the changing voltage from the amplifier's driver stage. Imagine that

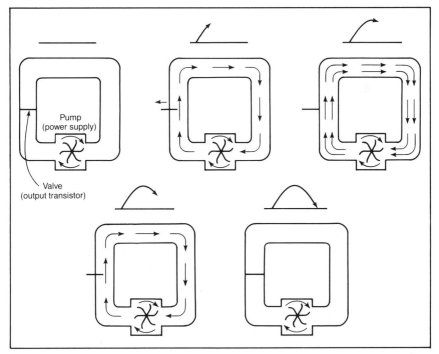

Power Output Stage. The output transistors (or tubes) of an amplifier operate like valves, varying the amount of current that flows from the power supply to the loudspeakers. The opening and closing of these electronic "valves" is controlled by the varying amplitude of the input voltage.

the input to the amplifier is a sine wave. The output transistors are arranged in pairs that handle each cycle in two halves. As the voltage from the amplifier's driver stage goes from 0 up to its maximum and down again, one half of each output pair "opens up" and "closes" again. When the voltage crosses the zero line and heads down, the first half of each pair passes off to the second, and then back again when the voltage again returns to the zero crossing. The wider the electronic valves open, the more current flows out of the power supply to the speaker.

Current and Power

The amount of current delivered also depends on the impedance of the loudspeaker. *Impedance* is the opposition of a circuit or component to the flow of electricity. Low impedances draw proportionately more current than high ones, following the formula $I = E/R$, where I is the current in amperes (amps), E is the voltage, and R is the resistance (or impedance) in ohms. Power (in watts) is equal to voltage times current ($P = EI$), which is equivalent to the voltage squared divided by the impedance ($P = E^2/R$). And the more power sent to a loudspeaker, the louder it will play.

At least, that's how it's supposed to work. In practice, the situation is more complicated. The voltage and current available from the power supply are not unlimited, and there are restrictions on the amount of current and power that the output transistors can handle, as well. Voltage limitations become apparent when the input to the power amplifier becomes so large that the amp can no longer provide as much output voltage as its gain demands. When this happens, the peaks of the signal are shorn off at the maximum voltage, generating large amounts of distortion. This condition is known as *overload,* or *clipping,* and depending on its severity and the design of the amplifier, its audible effect can range from a mild compression of the sound to harshness or raspiness. The basic power specification for every ampli-

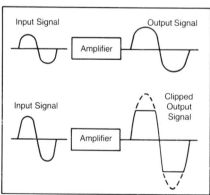

Clipping. Overload, or *clipping*, occurs when the input signal is too great for the amplifier to deliver a correspondingly large output. The result is an output signal that looks sheared off at the top or bottom, where the amplifier is hitting maximum power before the waveform can complete its excursion. This creates severe distortion.

fier is the amount of continuous power it can deliver into an 8-ohm resistive load over a specified frequency range with a specified level of distortion. Normally, the rated power is that which can be reached just short of clipping and is determined mainly by the amplifier's power-supply voltage.

At low impedances, however, current limitations come into play. The lower the load impedance, the greater the current (and therefore power) that will be drawn for a given voltage. Eventually a point will be reached where the power supply can no longer provide increasing amounts of current. What happens then is analogous to what happens when you open wide the nozzle on a garden hose: In the hose, the pressure drops, and in the amplifier, the voltage sags. So what you typically see in an amplifier is a pattern of increasing maximum power as the load impedance is reduced, until the power supply's current limit is approached and the output levels off (the exact shape of the power-vs.-impedance curve will depend on the design of the amplifier).

Another factor influencing amplifier power at low impedances is what's known as the *safe operating area* (SOA) of the output transistors. A few amplifiers use *FET* (field-effect transistor) outputs that simply won't pass more current than they can stand. But standard bipolar transistors of the kind used in the great majority of amplifiers will destroy themselves if asked to handle too much current for too long a time. For this reason, virtually all receivers and amplifiers include protection circuits to prevent such conditions from arising.

Typically, these circuits operate by sensing current flow or temperature and clamping the output voltage when necessary, which in turn reduces the current draw. The downside of such current-limiting circuits is that when they are activated they clip the amplifier, causing distortion. (Other protection measures might include fuses or thermally controlled cutoff devices.) And they can have other untoward effects, as well. Consequently, it is best that the output transistors be rugged enough to withstand as much current as they will ever need to pass to a loudspeaker.

This would be a relatively minor issue were it not for the fact that few speakers are simple resistive loads. Typically, they include reactive elements (inductances and capacitances) that cause their impedances to vary widely with frequency—often by a factor of 4 or 5 to 1. It is not uncommon for a speaker's impedance to drop to half or less its rated value at certain frequencies. So a receiver or amplifier may from time to time find itself called upon to provide far more current than the nominal impedance of the speakers that it is driving would suggest. If at all possible, find out how any receiver you are considering buying performs when driving low-impedance loads. Its power should certainly be as great into 4 ohms as into 8 ohms (preferably at least 50 percent higher), and respectable output into 2 ohms is another good sign. Magazine reviews usually include this information, and often it is listed on product specification sheets. If not, the dealer or manufacturer should be able to supply it to you on request.

Note, by the way, that some manufacturers have taken to quoting "peak current capability" figures and the like for their amps and receivers. This is fine, but since there is no standard governing the determination of these ratings, they are not necessarily comparable to one another. You're better off going by the power into low-impedance loads.

Headroom, Decibels, and All That

Continuous power is not the only measure of amplifier muscle. Another, often more relevant, one is its *dynamic* power—the output it can deliver in the short bursts characteristic of many musical peaks. The standard measurement for this is *dynamic headroom*, which is the amount by which the amplifier can exceed its continuous power rating on a train of 20-millisecond pulses, expressed in dB (decibels).

To make sense of dynamic headroom, and many other things we will be discussing in the course of this book, you need to understand the *decibel,* which is the most common unit of measure employed in audio. Technically, the difference in decibels between two signals is equal to 10 times the common logarithm of the ratio of their powers or 20 times the logarithm of the ratio of their voltages or currents. But you needn't worry about that. What's important for our purposes is that the decibel scale is a good match to the way we hear.

Watts vs. dBW. Amplifier power ratings are almost always given in watts, but you can better grasp the audible significance of power differences by using the dBW (decibel-watts) scale. A power increase of 10 dBW corresponds, approximately, to a doubling of perceived loudness; increases of less than 3 dBW seldom have much audible effect.

WATTS	dBW	WATTS	dBW
1.0	0	32	15
1.25	1	40	16
1.6	2	50	17
2.0	3	63	18
2.5	4	80	19
3.2	5	100	20
4.0	6	125	21
5.0	7	160	22
6.3	8	200	23
8.0	9	250	24
10.0	10	320	25
12.5	11	400	26
16.0	12	500	27
20.0	13	630	28
25.0	14	800	29

For example, let's suppose that we're driving a loudspeaker with a tone at 1 watt. Now we raise the level to 10 watts, which happens to be a change of 10 dB. To our ears, the volume will have about doubled. (Note that a tenfold increase does not yield a proportionate rise in perceived loudness—just a doubling.) Then we push the level up to 100 watts. That's another 10 dB, and again the tone sounds about twice as loud as before. As you can see, the decibel measurement is giving us a much better handle on the audible consequences of these changes than the power measurement.

Another handy rule of thumb is that a doubling of the power corresponds to a change of 3 dB. (A doubling of voltage or current is 6 dB.) So, if one amplifier is twice as powerful as another, that means it can play about 3 dB louder.

Now, back to dynamic headroom. If you see a receiver with a continuous power rating of 50 watts per channel and a dynamic headroom of 3 dB, that means it can deliver 100 watts per channel in brief spurts. On music, such a receiver will perform almost as well as one rated at 100 watts per channel continuously but with no dynamic headroom. In fact, you may find it worthwhile to compare mainly on the basis of dynamic power, which can be obtained by converting the continuous power rating in watts to a decibel scale (called *dBW*) and adding the dynamic headroom. We've even supplied a conversion chart to help you. You'll see that, per our example, 50 watts equals 17 dBW; adding 3 dB of dynamic headroom yields 20 dBW, or 100 watts, of dynamic power.

Class Distinctions

You may have noticed that some amplifiers are described as Class A, others as Class AB, and so forth. These categories are based on how the amps handle a basic design problem. As we've already mentioned, amplifiers normally use pairs of transistors, with one half handling the positive side of the signal, and the other, the negative side. Transistors tend to be very nonlinear at the point where they switch on or off—at

Switching Distortion. Crossover, or *switching*, distortion *(bottom)* occurs when a signal passes through the very nonlinear region near the point at which a transistor turns on or completely off. Class A and AB amplifiers reduce or eliminate switching distortion by applying a bias current to the transistors that keeps low-level signals out of the nonlinear area.

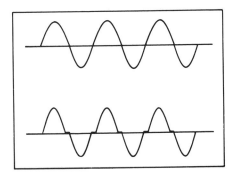

the juncture between signal and no signal. So left to their own devices, they produce "switching," or "crossover," distortion when the signal goes to 0 on its way positive from negative or negative from positive. This is the Class B mode of operation. It is efficient, but not very clean.

Class A amplifiers are at the opposite extreme. They operate their transistors with a constant DC bias current large enough to keep the transistors from ever turning entirely off. When there is no input signal, these bias currents are balanced, and there is no output. A signal will cause the current balance between the two sides to swing back and forth through the attached loudspeaker. Class A operation completely eliminates switching distortion, but it is very inefficient and generates large amounts of heat, requiring large, heavy heat sinks. Consequently, traditional Class A amplifiers tend to be low-power, expensive, or both, and you will not find any receivers that operate in this mode.

The standard solution to this dilemma is a compromise mode called Class AB, which uses enough bias for the amplifier to effectively operate as a Class A amp for small signals and as a Class B amp for large ones, on the theory that the large signals will mask any switching distortion. The result is an amplifier that is cleaner than Class B and more efficient than Class A. Until fairly recently, all receivers had Class AB power-amp sections.

A more elegant approach is embodied in *nonswitching,* or *sliding-bias,* amplifiers, which vary the bias according to the signal level. The idea is to keep the bias just large enough to prevent the transistors from ever switching off. Most of the time, the current required to achieve this is quite small. Only for signal peaks is a large bias current necessary. Like conventional Class A designs, nonswitching amplifiers produce no crossover distortion, yet they compare favorably with Class AB amps in cost and efficiency.

Volume and Balance

If a receiver's power-amp section is its muscle, its preamp stage is its brain. That's where all the control functions are located. The most fundamental of these are the volume and balance controls. Both affect signal level. The volume control raises or lowers the level by the same amount in both channels, whereas the balance control alters the level of the right channel relative to that of the left. For example, if you turn the balance control to the right, it will increase the level of the signal in the right channel and reduce that of the signal in the left. This will tend to move the stereo image to the right. Turning the balance control in the other direction has the opposite effect.

Like most other control functions that involve fine, continuous adjustments, volume and balance are best handled with knobs or slid-

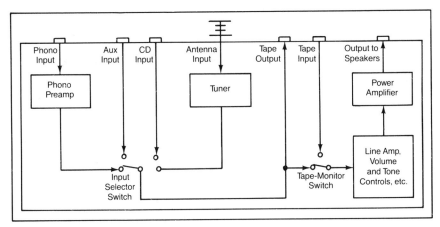

Signal Flow in an Audio Receiver

ers. Electronic push-button controls will work, but they tend to be harder to use, less precise, and slower.

Tone Controls, Equalizers, and Filters

A second major class of preamp controls are those that affect tonal balance. The most familiar of these are bass and treble controls, which enable you to boost or cut the low and high frequencies, respectively, to achieve a more pleasing sound. Many people seem to take extreme positions on the use of these controls. Some avoid them altogether, leaving them set to their middle positions no matter what the recording sounds like. Others set them both to maximum and leave them there no matter what the recording sounds like. The former approach probably makes more sense, but neither is ideal. Often a recording may benefit from a small touch-up: a slight treble cut to tame a tendency to harshness or shrillness, a mild bass boost to add warmth to a recording on which that quality is lacking, and so forth. As in most other matters audio or video, don't be afraid to experiment.

The main drawback of conventional tone controls is their lack of flexibility. What they can do may not address the exact problem you're encountering. One way tone controls can be made better is to make the frequencies at which they start working selectable. Some receivers and amplifiers offer two or three options for each control. A more aggressive approach is to add more controls. This can be as simple as putting in a midrange control (not usually all that worthwhile) or, it can be so thoroughgoing that you wind up with a built-in graphic equalizer covering five or more frequency bands. Once you get to that point, however, it usually makes more sense to buy a separate equalizer (more about that later). For a receiver or an integrated amp, variable-turnover tone controls probably represent the optimum balance

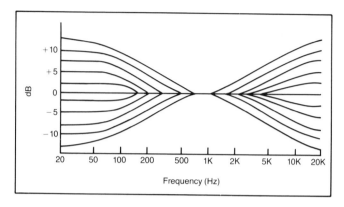

between ease of use and total adaptability.

In the similar-but-different category are filters. (Technically, tone controls and equalizers are filters, but the term more commonly is used to describe a circuit designed to completely eliminate some range of frequencies.) Filters used to be more common on audio equipment than they are today. As the 78-rpm record has faded into history and the CD has risen to dominance, the need for a high-cut (low-pass) hiss or scratch filter has almost disappeared. And the old-fashioned low-cut (high-pass) rumble filter, designed to attenuate low-frequency noise from the turntables of twenty or thirty years ago, has likewise become a feature mainly of the past.

But still valuable to those with record collections is a sharp infrasonic (often mislabeled "subsonic") filter to remove signals below the audible range generated by warped records, which can cause distortion and waste amplifier power. Sometimes an infrasonic filter is built into the phono preamp stage, or it may affect all inputs and be switchable from the front panel. Either way, look for a slope of at least 12 dB per octave and a cutoff around 15 or 20 Hz. Shallower slopes are not very effective and take a bite out of the audible range as well as that below.

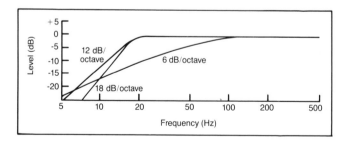

Filter Characteristics. Response curves for 6-, 12-, and 18-dB-per-octave low-cut (high-pass) filters demonstrate the greater precision and effectiveness of the high-order circuits. The 12- and (especially) 18-dB-per-octave slopes can be used to sharply attenuate unwanted infrasonic signals from warped records without affecting response within the audible band. The 6-dB-per-octave filter is both less effective and more intrusive.

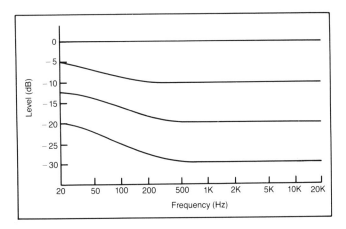

Loudness Compensation. A well-designed loudness-compensation control will attenuate low frequencies more gradually than high frequencies as you turn down the volume, to correct for the ear's loss of sensitivity in the bass range at low sound levels. Most alter the treble response as well, but this is not strictly correct practice.

Loudness Compensation

Most receivers and amplifiers have a loudness button. The function of this cryptically labeled switch is to activate a loudness-compensation circuit. Loudness compensation is supposed to correct for the ear's reduced sensitivity to bass frequencies at low levels. This is done by boosting the low end slightly relative to the rest of the range as the overall level is reduced. But since the amount of boost that should be applied for a given setting of the volume control varies according to a number of factors (such as loudspeaker sensitivity) not under the control of the receiver manufacturer, getting the compensation right is a rather tricky affair that requires a number of user adjustments. Some receivers, amps, and preamps make a stab in that direction, but most take a best-guess approach; and many boost the treble as well as the bass, which is simply wrong. All in all, you're usually best off acting as if the switch weren't there.

Mode Switching

Another near-universal feature is a mode switch of some kind. This can range from a simple stereo/mono button to a selector that offers such options as reverse stereo (left channel to right and right to left), either channel to both speakers, and so forth. The ability to switch to mono can be invaluable at times, so you should expect a switch for that purpose at minimum. Although the other possibilities described above are less essential, they are nonetheless handy at times for troubleshooting and are well worth having.

Inputs, Outputs, and In Between

Although it may seem so obvious as not to require explanation, one of the key features of a receiver is the ability to accept signals from a variety of sources and get them where you want them to go. A modern audio receiver normally will have four basic types of inputs: a tuner input, internally connected to the receiver's on-board tuner section; a phono input, for connection to a turntable; one or more "high-level," or "auxiliary," inputs, for things like CD players; and one or more tape inputs.

The phono input is special in that it feeds a dedicated preamplifier circuit designed to boost the tiny signals from a phono cartridge to a level similar to that from a CD player, tuner, or tape deck. It also provides an appropriate input impedance (usually vital for correct operation of the cartridge) and an inverse RIAA equalization network to undo the standard bass cut and treble boost applied in record mastering to prevent overcutting at low frequencies and reduce noise at high. Some units provide separate inputs or switchable gain to accommodate low-output moving-coil cartridges, which require even more amplification than regular cartridges. The output from the phono preamp

RIAA Phono Equalization. All modern phonograph records are made with boosted highs to overcome noise and reduced lows to prevent overcutting of the groove during disc mastering. Phono preamplifiers apply reciprocal equalization in playback to yield a net flat frequency response with low noise and undistorted bass.

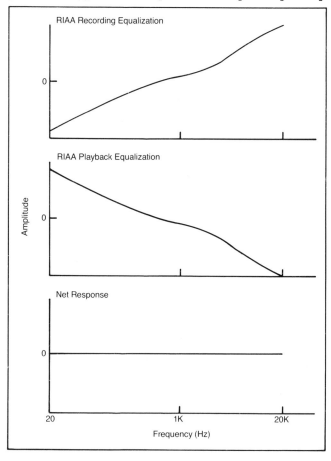

feeds into the source selector switch.

High-level and tuner inputs, on the other hand, go directly to the selector. And finally we come to the tape inputs, which usually are downstream from the main selector. They are paired with outputs to feed signals from the main selector to the inputs of the recorder. A monitor switch enables you to send either the feed from the main selector or the output from the tape deck on through the receiver to the speakers. (The path from tape output to deck and back from the deck to the tape inputs and the tape selector switch is called a *tape-monitor loop.* Alternatively, this path can be used to attach an external signal-processing unit, such as an equalizer.) This arrangement enables you to listen to the source chosen at the main selector, to a tape, or (if you have a three-head tape deck) to switch between the source being recorded and the output off the tape for comparison.

Many receivers have more than one tape-monitor loop, enabling you to copy from one deck to another. In the simplest arrangement, you can copy in only one direction, but more sophisticated schemes permit dubbing from either deck to the other. On some amplifiers and receivers, you can even copy from deck to deck while listening to another source. And the ultimate in flexibility is provided by amps and receivers that have a recording selector separate from the main source selector, so that you can record from any source while listening to any other (or the same one).

Only after it has passed through the receiver's various selector switches does the output from the chosen source make its way to the signal-modifying controls in the preamp stage (such as the volume, balance, and tone controls) and from there through the power amplifier to the speakers.

Speaker Switching

In a receiver or integrated amplifier, an audio signal's last way station usually is a switch that enables you to send it to any or all of perhaps as many as three pairs of speakers. (Some separate power amplifiers also have such a switch, but the feature is less common there.) This switch can make one of two kinds of connections: parallel or serial. A parallel connection attaches each selected pair directly to the same set of outputs, whereas a serial connection daisy-chains them, with the signal passing from one speaker to the next.

Although the preferable arrangement, parallel connection has one potentially serious drawback: The sum of impedances wired in parallel is smaller than any of the impedances taken alone. For example, the impedance an amplifier sees when two 8-ohm speakers are connected to it in parallel is 4 ohms. That can be a problem if you're trying to run more than one pair of low-impedance speakers at the same time from

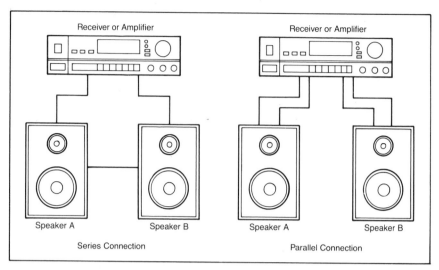

Serial and Parallel Speaker Connections. An amplifier can drive multiple pairs of speakers through either serial or parallel connections. (The connections are shown here as external for clarity; in practice, the connections are made inside the receiver or amplifier to simplify installation and facilitate switching.) The serial connection presents a higher-impedance, and therefore a less stressful, load to the amplifier, but it can cause frequency-response errors. Parallel is normally preferable.

an amplifier with modest current capability. In that case, you may have to limit the volume at which you listen when multiple speaker pairs are engaged or run only one set at a time.

Serially connected impedances add the way you would expect: 8 ohms plus 8 ohms equals 16 ohms, not 4. But for high-fidelity audio, it is not a good arrangement. The tonal balance (frequency response) of a speaker will change when it is driven with another speaker between it and the amplifier, as must be the case in a serial connection. And if the speaker is at all good, that change surely will be for the worse. An easy way to test for serially connected speaker switching is to select an unused speaker output while speakers are playing from another. If the connection is parallel, the music will continue; if it is serial, the missing speaker will open the connection and the music will stop.

Audio-Video Receivers

When people first began trying to integrate their audio and video systems, one of the biggest problems they faced was tying all the equipment together in a way that made sense. Having to find and flip half a dozen switches to go from an audio source to a video source or vice versa is not a step in the direction of convenience. Only when audio-video amplifiers and receivers became available did everything start falling into place.

The principal distinguishing feature of audio-video amps and receivers is routing and switching of video as well as audio signals. On

An Audio-Video Receiver

the back panel, you will find a number of inputs and outputs with three jacks instead of the usual two: left-channel audio, right-channel audio, and video. Now you can attach a laser videodisc player (or CD/CD-V/LD player), a VCR or two, and your video monitor as well as your speakers, turntable, cassette deck, and other audio components. If you select the videodisc player, its audio output will go to your speakers; its video output, to the monitor. And if you like, you can record from it to a VCR while you are watching. You may even be able to copy from disc or another VCR while you view or listen to another source, or record video from one source and audio from another—all with minimum fuss (and therefore maximum enjoyment).

Simulated Stereo

Although appropriate switching is a big part of the appeal of an audio-video amplifier or receiver, it is not the whole story. Most include other features designed specifically to enhance the audio-video experience. Perhaps the most common is a switchable simulated-stereo circuit for use with video sources that have mono soundtracks. The idea is to add a sense of spaciousness to the typically closed-in sound of mono. Whether this sort of treatment is appropriate or sounds good to you will depend on your tastes and the nature of the soundtrack. Simulated stereo works by spreading out the mono sound; it cannot create a true stereo image.

Surround Sound

Less common but far more interesting is built-in surround-sound processing, primarily for Dolby Stereo movie soundtracks. Dolby Stereo is more than its name might imply, since it conveys not only standard left/right stereo, but also a center channel for dialogue and a surround

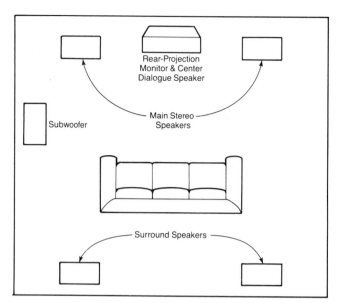

Room Layout for a Typical Dolby Surround System

Rear-Projection Monitor & Center Dialogue Speaker

Subwoofer

Main Stereo Speakers

Surround Speakers

channel for spatial effects (helicopters flying overhead, twigs cracking behind you, and so forth). The prints used by most theaters and for transfer to laser videodisc and tape have these two additional channels of information matrix-encoded into the two main stereo channels. The center-channel sound is mixed in as a mono (L + R) signal, and the surround sound goes in as a difference signal (L − R) with Dolby B noise reduction. With proper decoding, the soundtracks on these prints will deliver the realism-enhancing surround effect for which Dolby Stereo has become famous. In the absence of such decoding, however, they will play back in normal stereo.

Dolby Laboratories sanctions two levels of Dolby Stereo decoding for the home. The simpler and more common (especially in audio-video amps and receivers) is called *Dolby Surround.* This process simply extracts the surround channel, runs it through a Dolby B noise-reduction chip, delays it fifteen to thirty milliseconds, and sends it to one or more speakers at the back of the room. (Although there is only a single channel of surround information, it usually sounds better if it is reproduced from more than one location.)

Although simple Dolby Surround decoding can give exciting results, it does not duplicate the advanced, high-performance processing used in movie theaters. For that, you need *Dolby Pro Logic* decoding. Pro Logic adds a couple of significant elements to the system. One is center-channel extraction, which is important for anchoring dialogue at the middle of the stereo stage. And often a subwoofer output is provided for improved reproduction of the extremely low frequencies used in some motion-picture sound effects. The other is logic steering, which works to reduce leakage between channels. For example, in basic Dolby Surround decoding, pure difference-signal (L − R) information goes to the front stereo channels as well as the rear surround; in Pro Logic, it goes strictly to the back. This quite noticeably improves the quality of the surround-sound effect. Although Pro Logic used to be the province solely of outboard decoders, it is now beginning to make its way into audio-video amplifiers and receivers.

Video Enhancement

Signal processing need not be limited to audio. In fact, you can do some pretty spectacular things with video if you have the right equipment. On an audio-video receiver, however, the processing feature you're most likely to find is a sharpness control or video enhancer. These vary in sophistication, but the intent is to sharpen edges and bring out details that tend to get softened or lost in recording to a VCR. Like any other kind of signal processing, video enhancement can make things worse if overused. Carefully applied, however, it can be a real benefit, especially if you do a lot of dubbing from tape to tape.

A Word (or Two) About Specifications

The first time a person goes out to shop for high-quality audio or video equipment, he or she may be surprised at the extensive engineering specifications supplied by manufacturers for their products. This information can be exceedingly useful if you know what to look for. Otherwise, you may simply find it offputting. Throughout this book, we will be helping you understand what the specifications for the various components mean and how to use them in deciding what to buy. In particular, we will provide a brief explanatory rundown of the relevant specifications for each type of component at the end of the chapter devoted to it.

But before we move on to the list for receivers, let's pause to examine in detail a few important specifications that cut across categories: signal-to-noise ratio (S/N), distortion, frequency response, and channel separation.

Noise

Taken together, noise and distortion account for everything unintentionally added to a signal as it passes through the recording and playback chains. They differ only in their correlation to the signal. Noise normally is taken to comprise additions that are independent of the signal. (There are two exceptions to this rule: modulation noise in analog tape recording and quantization noise in digital audio, both of which vary according to the signal.) Its most common forms are hiss and hum. *Hiss* is random or nearly random sound that is produced in at least small amounts by all electronic components. *Hum* arises from electromagnetic induction of the AC power-line frequency (60 Hz in North America) into an audio cable or circuit. Usually it can be traced to a power cord or to the magnetic field emanating from a power transformer. Both hiss and hum can be minimized through good design.

Noise specifications are stated in the form of *signal-to-noise ratios*. This is simply the amount, in decibels, by which a signal at a standard test level exceeds the level of noise produced by a component. So all else being equal, the higher the S/N, the better. The test signal depends on the type of component being tested. For example, the current IHF/EIA amplifier testing standard requires that the S/N of power amplifiers be measured with an input signal that yields a 1-watt output. Before this standard came into effect, it was common for amplifier S/N to be specified relative to full rated power. A moment's thought will reveal how misleading this could be, since full output for a 100-watt amplifier is 6 dB greater than that for a 25-watt amp.

Because our ears are less sensitive to very low and very high frequencies than to sounds in between, audio noise measurements should be weighted to account for this effect: Noise at 50 Hz or 10 kHz should count less than noise at 1 kHz, for example. If no weighting is used, it is possible for a component with a high signal-to-noise ratio to sound noisier than one with a slightly lower S/N. The method most commonly used in audio measurements is called *A-weighting*.

S/N measurements are also important in video, where noise appears as "snow" *(luminance noise)* or as an unstable mottled quality in large fields of color *(chroma noise)*.

Distortion

Unlike noise, distortion does depend on the input signal. There are two basic types of distortion: harmonic and intermodulation. Harmonic distortion consists of spurious signals at frequencies that are multiples of the one desired. That is, the second-harmonic distortion product from a 1-kHz signal is at 2 kHz, the third-harmonic product is at 3 kHz, and so on. The RMS (root-mean-square) sum of all the individual harmonic-distortion components is called the *total harmonic distortion* (THD). THD is the single most commonly quoted distortion specification.

A variant of THD is THD + N, or total harmonic distortion *plus noise*. This measurement is a summation of all the components in the output from a device that are not part of the desired signal.

Intermodulation (IM) distortion consists of the sum and difference products generated when two or more signals pass through a component. For example, signals at 100 Hz and 1 kHz would yield sum and difference products of 1.1 kHz and 900 Hz, respectively. Any device that produces harmonic distortion also produces IM distortion, and vice versa, normally in similar proportions. Although IM measurements are necessary in some cases, THD tests usually are adequate if they are performed across the entire audio band.

Distortion figures can be (and sometimes are) expressed in the same way as signal-to-noise ratios—as the ratio, in decibels, of the amplitude of the desired signal or signals to the amplitude of the distortion products. But they usually are given as percentages. For example, 1% THD would indicate that the RMS sum of the amplitudes of all the harmonic distortion components is equal to 1 percent of the amplitude of the desired signal.

In any component, distortion performance varies according to the frequencies and amplitudes of the signals. And the audibility of the distortion depends on the program material and the characteristics of the distortion products. When distortion does reach audible levels, it usually is heard as harshness, added warmth, or some other alteration of tonal balance. With modern equipment, this sort of coloration is rare.

Frequency Response

The influence of an audio system on the tonal balance of sound reproduced through it is determined almost exclusively by what is known as its *frequency response.* One aspect of frequency response is extension: the highest and lowest sounds that a system or component can reproduce. Although rather optimistic at the top for most people out of their teens, the range of human hearing generally is taken as 20 Hz to 20 kHz, and most audio components are specified on that basis. However, a range of about 30 Hz to 15 kHz is adequate for music reproduction. That is because normal music contains virtually no energy outside that range, and even people with excellent ears hear poorly at the frequency extremes.

Flat vs. Nonflat Response. A straight horizontal line across a graph of frequency versus amplitude indicates perfectly flat frequency response, which usually is the ideal. Peaks and dips in a response curve indicate emphasis and loss at those frequencies, corresponding to alterations in tonal balance.

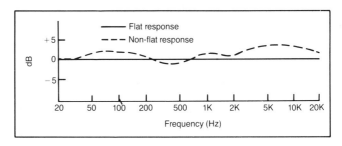

The idea of dismissing what appears to be nearly a quarter of the audible band usually disturbs people until they understand a certain peculiarity of human perception: We hear in octaves. An *octave* is a frequency range that defines a ratio of 2 to 1: 20 Hz to 40 Hz, 40 Hz to 80 Hz, 80 Hz to 160 Hz, and so on. Each of those intervals is an octave. If you sweep a tone up or down in frequency, you'll notice a cyclic quality to the sound. This occurs because tones at octave intervals sound like the same note at different pitches: High C sounds like a higher-pitched version of middle C, for example. They tend to sound more alike than tones that are nearer in frequency but not at some multiple of an octave away.

This has certain interesting consequences. One of them is that the range of 1.25–2.5 kHz, for example, is comparable, perceptually, to the range of 10–20 kHz. Each represents an octave. That last 5 kHz between 15 and 20 kHz amounts to less than half an octave in the approximately ten-octave range of the entire audio band.

The other important aspect of frequency response is evenness. The relative levels of different frequencies in the input signal should be preserved in the output. For example, if tones at 500 Hz and 10 kHz go in at the same level, they should come out at the same level. Similarly, if the 10-kHz signal goes in 4 dB lower than the 500-Hz one, it should come out 4 dB lower. When high tones are emphasized relative to low ones, the sound tends to be bright; when they are diminished, the sound becomes dull or muffled.

Frequency response can be stated in two ways. The more informative is the graphical approach, in which frequency (in Hz) is plotted horizontally on a chart and level (in dB) is plotted vertically. A signal of a known, constant level is fed into the component or system under test at all frequencies within the limits of interest (usually 20 Hz to 20 kHz). The output level is then measured and plotted for each frequency. From the resulting line, you can tell at a glance which frequencies the system is exaggerating and which it is attenuating, and by how much. Stating the maximum variation over the test frequency range (± 1 dB from 20 Hz to 20 kHz, for example) is simpler, but less revealing: You know the magnitude of the error, but not where it occurs.

Frequency response is among the most important audio specifications because we are acutely sensitive to it—even to variations as small as a few tenths of a dB in some cases. Clearly, the ideal would be something like ± 0 dB from 30 Hz to 15 kHz, corresponding to a straight horizontal line across the response chart (that is, "flat" frequency response). In practice, however, most audio components fall short of perfection. This is especially true of devices such as microphones, phono cartridges, and loudspeakers, which convert mechanical energy to electrical or vice versa.

Frequency response also comes up in video, though with a differ-

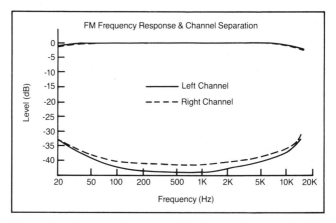

ent significance. There it relates to how much information can be displayed horizontally across the screen—what is known as the *horizontal resolution.* For the NTSC television system used in North America, Japan, and some other parts of the world, each megahertz of usable video bandwidth translates to approximately 80 lines of horizontal resolution.

Channel Separation

What fundamentally distinguishes a stereo signal from a mono one is the presence of two distinct audio channels carrying significantly different information. If there is too much mixture between them, the stereo effect will be lost. How well a component keeps the signals in the two channels apart is defined by its *channel separation.* Channel separation figures are obtained by feeding a signal into one channel only and measuring the difference (in decibels) between the output from that channel and from the other. The less leakage, or *crosstalk,* between channels, the better the channel separation.

Channel separation usually varies with frequency and is most important in the range of approximately 200 Hz and 5 kHz. For many components, channel separation is not much of an issue, since figures of 20–30 dB in that band are adequate for full stereo effect. For tuners and phono cartridges, however, it can be a matter of concern.

Tuner Specifications

The following brief explanations are applicable both to separate tuners and to the tuner sections built into receivers. They assume that the specifications are based on the 1976 IHF/EIA tuner-measurement standard, which mandates a signal strength of 65 dBf (decibel femtowatts) at the antenna terminals for most tests. That is great enough to assure full limiting on most component-quality tuners.

Sensitivity

The signal strength required to achieve a signal-to-noise ratio of 50 dB, also known as *50-dB quieting sensitivity*. (You may still see the older, less stringent "usable sensitivity" specification, which is based on 30-dB quieting. Despite its name, it is not very useful and should be ignored.) Lower numbers are better. In rare cases, a tuner may achieve sensitivities approaching 12 dBf in mono and 35 dBf in stereo (without blend), but 15–16 dBf in mono and around 38 dBf in stereo are more common. A decent component tuner should be able to achieve at least 40-dBf sensitivity in stereo.

Signal-to-Noise Ratio (S/N)

The amount by which a full-modulation signal exceeds the background noise level at a signal strength of 65 dBf. Larger numbers are better. Reasonable figures are 65 dB in stereo and 70 dB in mono. An outstandingly quiet tuner might achieve more than 70 dB in stereo and nearly 80 dB in mono.

Selectivity

A measure of how well a tuner discriminates against signals on channels close to the one you've tuned. Higher numbers are better. The figure normally reported is for alternate-channel selectivity, indicating how completely broadcasts two channels (400 kHz) away are rejected. A rating of 40–50 dB usually is adequate. Adjacent-channel selectivity—the ability to suppress stations only one channel (200 kHz) away—usually is much lower. Unless special attention is paid in the design of the tuner, it normally will be less than 10 dB. High adjacent-channel selectivity is beneficial only in exceptional circumstances and usually comes at some cost to other performance characteristics, such as distortion and channel separation.

Capture Ratio

Indicator of how well a tuner suppresses the weaker of two signals received on the same channel. Lower numbers are better. Capture ratio is the most important indicator of a tuner's resistance to multipath. At worst, it should be about 2 dB; 1 dB is outstanding.

AM Suppression

A tuner's ability to block out interfering amplitude-modulated signals from car ignitions, fluorescent lights, and so forth. Such noise also can be generated by multipath interference. Higher numbers are better, with 40 dB representing bare-minimum performance. A rating of 50 dB is more reasonable, and 60 dB or more is excellent.

Spurious-Response Rejection

A general indicator of a tuner's ability to reject signals at frequencies other than the one to which it is tuned. In particular, a signal strong enough to overload a tuner's front-end electronics may appear at multiple places on the dial. Higher numbers are better. Look for a minimum of 60 or 70 dB; some tuners are capable of more than 100 dB of spurious-response rejection.

IF Rejection

How well a tuner rejects external signals at its 10.7-MHz intermediate frequency. A tuner's rating here usually is close to that for spurious-response rejection, and again, higher numbers are better, with 60 or 70 dB representing acceptable performance.

Image Rejection

Indicator of a tuner's ability to suppress transmissions at twice its intermediate frequency—21.4 MHz. Higher numbers are better, and usually they are close to those for spurious-response and IF rejection. Image rejection usually is not too important unless you live near an airport, but expect a minimum of 60–70 dB.

Pilot and Subcarrier Rejection

FM reception typically involves a number of signals in addition to the audio baseband modulation. For stereo, these include a 19-kHz pilot tone to trigger the stereo demodulators in receivers and the 38-kHz stereo subcarrier. In addition, some stations broadcast unrelated information on a 67-kHz SCA subcarrier. To minimize audible side effects, all these signals (especially the 19-kHz pilot) should be filtered out of the audio signal. This is particularly important if the signal is to be recorded on a tape deck that uses Dolby noise reduction. Higher numbers are better. Look for at least 40, preferably 50, decibels of attenuation; 70 dB or more is excellent.

Distortion

For FM tuners, total harmonic distortion (THD) is measured at three frequencies: 100 Hz, 1 kHz, and 6 kHz. In addition, you may see figures for intermodulation (IM) distortion, which usually are comparable to those for THD. Figures of 0.5 percent or less are reasonable for typical modes of operation. All tuners will produce less distortion in mono than in stereo. Switching a tuner to its narrow IF mode, if it has one, will produce higher distortion. The exact amount will depend on how sharp the narrow-mode IF filters are, but distortion may reach 1 percent or more in stereo if the tuner has been designed for very high selectivity at this setting.

Frequency Response
The filter used to remove the 19-kHz stereo pilot tone may drop the response at 15 kHz by 2 or 3 dB, but apart from that, it should be within ± 1 dB from 30 Hz up to nearly 15 kHz. The best tuners have almost perfectly flat response over that range.

Channel Separation
Separation normally is greatest at midband, where it is most important. Ratings of 30 dB at 1 kHz and 15 dB at 10 kHz in normal operating mode are more than adequate. Figures 5–10 dB greater than that rank as excellent. Switching to a narrow IF setting, if one is available, will reduce overall separation somewhat, and FM noise-reduction systems typically reduce separation when they are in operation, especially at high frequencies.

Amplifier Specifications

Continuous Average Power
The maximum output an amplifier can deliver continuously into a specified load over a specified frequency range with no more than a specified amount of distortion. For example, a typical continuous-power rating might read "50 watts per channel, minimum, into 8 ohms from 20 Hz to 20 kHz with no more than 0.1% distortion." A continuous-power specification that does not contain all this information (which the Federal Trade Commission requires for home amplifiers and receivers) should be viewed with suspicion. It is easy to get higher power figures by permitting a large amount of distortion, for example. Sometimes subsidiary ratings are given for 4 or even 2 ohms, as well, which can be very useful information. Power should increase into lower impedances.

Dynamic Headroom and Power
The amount by which an amplifier can exceed its continuous-power rating in short bursts, such as those demanded by musical peaks. Figures of 1–3 dB are typical; more than that is rare. Dynamic headroom can be added to the continuous-power rating to obtain dynamic power. For example, an amplifier specified at 50 watts of continuous power with 3 dB of dynamic headroom would have a dynamic-power rating of 100 watts.

Signal-to-Noise Ratio (S/N)
The outcome of a noise measurement on an amplifier depends a great deal on how the test is performed. We will assume adherence to the 1978 IHF/EIA amplifier testing standard, which requires

specific input and output loads and levels and A-weighting of all measurements to assure realistic and comparable results. Higher numbers are better. Figures of about 75 dB for phono inputs and near 80 dB or greater for high-level inputs (CD, tape, and so forth) are typical and good enough that you are unlikely to hear noise from the amplifier itself under normal circumstances.

Distortion

Usually you will find that only total harmonic distortion (THD) is specified, but this is okay since the intermodulation (IM) figures almost invariably are quite similar. Lower numbers are better. A good modern amplifier will exhibit less than 0.1 percent distortion at any output level up to full power across the entire audio band (20 Hz to 20 kHz). This is low enough to be completely inaudible.

Frequency Response

Through its high-level inputs, an amplifier's response should be flat within a small fraction of a decibel across the audio band (20 Hz to 20 kHz). This assures that the amplifier will not alter the tonal balance of line-level signals passing through it (unless you use the tone controls to change it on purpose). You may see specifications that indicate response extending well beyond those limits, which is fine, but it is not necessary in any way.

Because of the RIAA equalization network required for correct playback of records, response through the phono input almost never is as flat as through the high-level section alone. At worst, it should be within ± 1 dB from 30 Hz to 15 kHz, and a good amplifier will hold the variance to ± 0.5 dB. A tolerance of approximately ± 0.2 dB from 20 Hz to 20 kHz is about the best that can be obtained.

Phono Overload

The largest signal the phono input can accept without clipping and generating gross distortion. Higher numbers are better. A phono-overload rating at 1 kHz of 100 millivolts (mV) for moving-magnet (MM) cartridges or about 10 millivolts for moving-coil (MC) pickups is more than adequate.

Input Impedance

In general, input impedances should be much greater than the output impedances of the devices feeding them. For high-level audio sources, such as Compact Disc players, output impedances seldom exceed 2,000 (2k) ohms and usually are 1,000 ohms or less. Consequently, an amplifier input impedance of 10,000–20,000 ohms normally is adequate. Values typically range from 10,000 to 100,000 ohms, with 20,000–50,000 being most common.

The situation for phono inputs is more complicated, as moving-magnet (MM) pickups normally expect to see a resistance within 5 or 10 percent of 47,000 ohms in parallel with some fairly specific capacitance, usually somewhere between 250 and 450 picofarads (pF). Incorrect loading will cause frequency-response errors. Adjustable input capacitance is a nice, but increasingly uncommon, feature. Failing that, a value of 100–200 picofarads is a good compromise, taking into account the capacitance of most tonearm cables. Moving-coil (MC) cartridges are much less sensitive to loading; anything greater than about 100 ohms should do.

Damping Factor

The impedance of the loudspeaker divided by the output impedance of the power amplifier. Normally, the measurement is taken at 50 Hz with an 8-ohm load. Theoretically, a high damping factor is better than a low one, but in practice, there's seldom any advantage to making it greater than 20 or so.

Video Specifications

Frequency Response

The video bandwidth should be great enough to pass unaltered any standard NTSC signal. At best, the upper frequency limit of such a signal might lie somewhere between 4.2 and 5 MHz. Therefore, response should be essentially flat to 5 or 6 MHz.

Signal-to-Noise Ratio (S/N)

To assure that video signals pass through the receiver without degradation, its video S/N should be at least 50 dB and preferably somewhat greater.

Crosstalk

To prevent interference between video inputs, leakage between them should be −50 to −55 dB or less.

Chapter 3

Loudspeakers

Loudspeakers

Though simple in appearance and operation, a loudspeaker has the very difficult job of converting electrical signals back into sound waves. Ideally, it would do this without altering frequency response or adding distortion, but the mechanical elements needed to set air in motion cannot be controlled as precisely as electrons flowing through transistors. And because a loudspeaker sprays energy over a wide angle into the room in which it is placed, its sound depends partly on the acoustic properties of that room and how the speaker interacts with them. Thus, not only does every model of loudspeaker sound different from every other model, but every speaker will also sound different depending on the room in which it is used and where in that room it is placed. The result of all this is that the loudspeakers in your system will have a greater effect on its sound than any other component.

Not surprisingly, then, you must choose your speakers carefully. Although the final selection should be based on listening, an understanding of how loudspeakers work and of the basic types of designs available can get you going in the right direction.

Drivers, Crossovers, and Systems

Almost invariably, what we refer to as a *loudspeaker* really comprises a number of individual speakers, called *drivers,* mounted together in

A Three-Way Loudspeaker

some kind of cabinet and linked by an electrical network that apportions the signal among them. Such a loudspeaker system uses two or more drivers tailored to specific frequency ranges. For example, low frequencies usually are handled by big, rugged woofers that can move the large amounts of air needed to reproduce long wavelengths at high levels. High frequencies normally go to a much smaller driver that can move fast enough to keep up with them.

The division between them is accomplished by what is known as a *crossover* (or dividing) network: a set of filters between the input to the loudspeaker and the drivers. In a two-way system, for example, the crossover network is a pair of filters. One, feeding the woofer, removes information above a certain frequency, while the other, connected to the tweeter, cuts off below that frequency. This point of intersection is called the *crossover frequency.*

Because the filters attenuate response gradually, rather than abruptly, there is some sharing of responsibility by the drivers in the vicinity of the crossover frequency. The width of this region of blended output is determined by the filter slopes, which are given in decibels per octave. In other words, a filter that rolls off at 6 dB per octave above 1.5 kHz will reduce its output relative to that at 1.5 kHz by 6 dB at 3 kHz, 12 dB at 6 kHz, 18 dB at 12 kHz, and so on. Crossover slopes range (with rare exceptions) from 6 dB to 24 dB per octave, depending on the design of the speaker.

Cutaway View of a Conventional Two-Way Box Loudspeaker

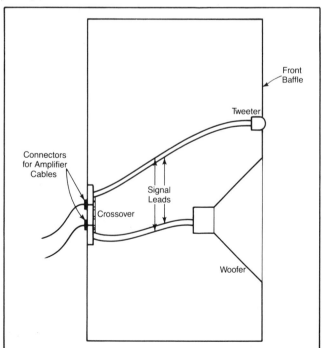

Front Baffle

Tweeter

Connectors for Amplifier Cables

Signal Leads

Crossover

Woofer

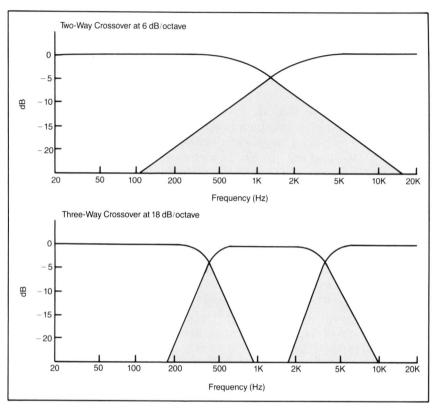

Crossover Characteristics. These graphs show fairly typical crossover filter responses for a two-way and a three-way speaker. The shading indicates regions of overlap between the outputs of the drivers. Speakers that split the band into three or more segments usually employ steeper crossover slopes to minimize interference between drivers.

Two-Way, Three-Way, or More?

Crossover-network design is at the heart of making a good loudspeaker. The best drivers in the world will not save a speaker from a crossover that produces rough transitions between them or that forces them to operate in ranges where their frequency response is poor or they are prone to distortion. Beware, however, of buying a design rather than a sound. The best crossover for a loudspeaker is the one that results in the best performance. Just knowing the crossover frequencies and slopes, for example, will not tell you whether they are appropriate.

The same warning applies to the number of drivers or crossovers used. A popular misconception is that a three-way speaker, with separate drivers for low, middle, and high frequencies, is always better than a two-way, which splits the audio band into just two ranges. (Some two-way systems actually have three or more drivers: two medium-size woofers in place of a single large one, for example, covering the same frequency range. Or you might encounter a three-way with multiple drivers for certain ranges, and so on.) There can be advantages to three-way—even four- or five-way—speaker systems, but their additional drivers and complex crossover networks make them harder to design and costlier to build. Some of the world's finest speakers have been two-ways, and at low and moderate prices, a good example of the breed is almost certain to be your best choice.

Types of Drivers

Loudspeaker drivers come in a bewildering array of shapes, sizes, and operating principles. The most common use cone or dome diaphragms made of paper, plastic, metal, or even ceramic. These *dynamic drivers,* as they are called, are basically electric motors. The apex of the cone or the rim of the dome is attached to a cylindrical former around which are wrapped many turns of wire. This structure, known as a *voice coil,* fits into a narrow circular gap in a strong permanent magnet. The magnet is at the rear of a supporting frame called a *basket.* The edge of the cone or dome is secured to the front of the basket by a flexible surround that permits the diaphragm to move fore and aft in a controlled fashion.

Output from an amplifier passes through a speaker system's crossover network to the voice coils of the drivers. The current flowing through a voice coil induces a magnetic field whose strength and polarity vary according to the fluctuating signal level. This field interacts

Cutaway View of a Typical Moving-Coil Woofer. Signal current from the amplifier flows through the voice-coil wire, inducing a varying magnetic field. The interaction of that field with the fixed field of the driver's magnet assembly forces the cone to move back and forth, generating sound waves in the air.

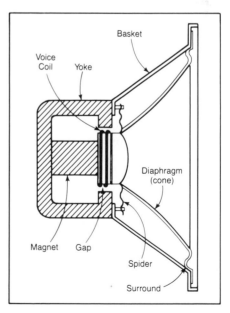

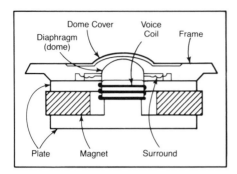

Cutaway View of a Dome Tweeter

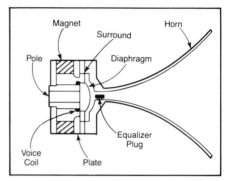

Cutaway View of a Horn Tweeter. Horn loading increases driver efficiency, allowing high output levels with relatively low power input.

with the constant field from the permanent magnet, pushing the coil back and forth in the magnet's gap. Since the cone or dome is attached to the voice coil, it goes along for the ride, creating vibrations in the air. This is how nearly all loudspeakers make sound.

Electrostatics, Ribbons, and Other Alternatives

Dynamic drivers have earned their popularity with a combination of cost, performance, and reliability that is hard to beat. But they do have competition.

Perhaps the best-known alternative is the *electrostatic driver.* The diaphragm of an electrostatic is an ultrathin sheet of plastic impregnated with some conductive material and stretched taut in front of or (usually) between perforated metal plates. It is charged with a constant DC voltage, supplied by a transformer that plugs into an AC wall socket. In a push-pull electrostatic, the two plates are connected to the positive and negative amplifier outputs. The audio signal from the amp creates charges on these plates that force the diaphragm to move back and forth by electrostatic attraction and repulsion.

Electrostatic drivers have certain appealing qualities, including low distortion and flat, extended high-frequency response. Their main weaknesses tend to be in efficiency, power handling, directivity, and sometimes reliability. Electrostatic forces fall off rapidly with distance (following the inverse-square law), which encourages the designer to put the plates as close as possible to the diaphragm without interfering with its motion. Unfortunately, that greatly increases the risk of arcing. But backing the plates off from the diaphragm reduces efficiency, so that more power is required from the amplifier to obtain a given acoustic output. The directivity problem arises from the tendency of electrostatic elements to be fairly large, which reduces dispersion. Most electrostatic speakers force you to sit within a fairly small area for best sound.

Despite their drawbacks, electrostatic loudspeakers have loyal adherents among serious audiophiles. And no wonder, for some of the world's great loudspeakers have been based on this principle.

Some designers have attempted to sidestep the problems of electrostatics by building similar speakers with electromagnetic drivers. These are, in effect, distributed-voice-coil dynamic loudspeakers. Wire is threaded through a thin plastic diaphragm stretched in front of or between rows of permanent magnets and attached to the amplifier outputs. Signal current from the amplifier induces a varying magnetic field in the wire that interacts with the constant magnetic field, causing the diaphragm to vibrate back and forth with the music. The diaphragm mass of such speakers tends to be greater than for comparable electrostatics, sometimes impairing high-frequency response. But they usually have the edge in power handling and efficiency, en-

Side View of an Electrostatic Driver. The signal from the amplifier varies the electrical charges on the stators. Electrostatic attraction and repulsion between these varying charges and the fixed charge on the diaphragm cause the diaphragm to move back and forth, creating sound.

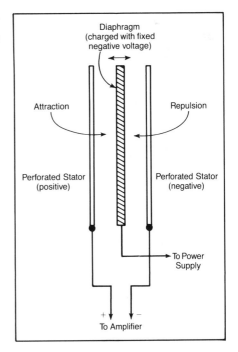

abling them to play louder without risk of damage. They also are an easier load for an amplifier and more often are manufactured in the form of small drivers with good high-frequency dispersion. And you don't have to plug them in.

The third major (if it can be called that) alternative to ordinary dynamic drivers is the *ribbon loudspeaker,* which is similar in concept to the planar-magnetic speakers described above. The main difference is that the diaphragm is a thin, conductive metal foil. Historically, ribbons have been fragile and inefficient, but there has been a lot of work on them in recent years, which has yielded significant improvements.

Sizes and Shapes

The size and shape of a dynamic driver are determined mainly by the frequency range it must reproduce. For low frequencies, fairly large cone drivers are appropriate because of their ability to move large amounts of air and to take a lot of power without sustaining damage (most of the energy in music is below 500 Hz or so). At high frequencies, however, their output tends to become ragged and attenuated. And at frequencies high enough for the wavelength to be small relative to the diameter of the cone, the angle over which sound is radiated will become undesirably narrow. This is why the woofers in two-way systems, which must work up to the low end of a small tweeter, seldom are larger than eight inches in diameter.

To reproduce high frequencies smoothly and with reasonably wide dispersion, a tweeter must be small. Fortunately, it doesn't have to make large excursions or handle large amounts of power. Tweeter diaphragms seldom exceed two inches in diameter, and most are domes. The reason domes are preferred has little to do with sound distribution, by the way; that is determined primarily by the driver's size. It is simply that a small dome can be made more rigid than a cone, which helps maintain smooth frequency response and low distortion. Such small drivers do not function well at low frequencies. Their output falls off, and they begin to distort badly as they are pushed beyond their excursion limits. The lower useful limit of a typical one-inch dome tweeter is between 1.5 kHz and 2 kHz.

A three-way speaker uses an in-between-size driver—usually between two and five inches across—called a *midrange.* This saves the woofer and tweeter from having to operate at the limits of their frequency ranges, where their performance is beginning to weaken. In a typical system, the woofer might work up to about 500 Hz and the tweeter down to approximately 3 kHz, with the midrange driver bridging the gap. Three-ways put a premium on the design of the crossover network, which usually must employ steeper filter slopes than are common in two-way systems. Otherwise, the outputs of the drivers may overlap too much and interfere with each other. This costs money and makes life harder for the engineers, but in return you may get lower distortion and sometimes smoother frequency response in the range where the ear is most sensitive.

Materials

The last five years have seen increasing use of new and exotic materials in the construction of dynamic drivers. These have included plastics, such as polypropylene, sometimes reinforced with carbon fiber or other substances to enhance rigidity; metals (copper, aluminum, beryllium, and titanium); and, most recently, ceramics. Every new direction is an attempt to achieve a better balance of mass, rigidity, and internal damping of resonances. Again, though, it is best not to get too carried away by the technology. What counts are the results, not the means used to obtain them. Ironically, one of the best diaphragm materials is still paper, but it does not afford the manufacturing consistency of the plastics that increasingly have supplanted it.

A Baffling Experience

The one part of a loudspeaker that we have not discussed so far is the cabinet. Although a loudspeaker enclosure has the obvious task of holding all the parts of the system together in the correct relationship to one another, it performs other important functions as well. One of them is solving an important problem in bass reproduction. Even a large woofer will have disappointing low-frequency output if you just put it out on a table and try to play music through it. This is because the driver produces sound waves from both its front and back surfaces, but 180 degrees out of phase with each other. At low frequencies, where wavelengths are long relative to the size of the driver, the sound waves will bend around the edge of the cone and partially cancel each other.

The straightforward approach to preventing such cancellation is to mount the woofer on a large surface, called a *baffle,* so that even long wavelengths will not wrap around and annihilate each other. But unless you build your speakers into a wall (an increasingly popular option these days), this technique has some serious practical limitations. Usually a moderate-size baffle is used as the front surface of a cabinet that traps most of the backwave from the woofer. One of the important differences among loudspeakers is what their enclosures do with this trapped sound.

Infinite Baffles and Acoustic Suspension

One approach is to approximate a true infinite baffle by using a large woofer in a large sealed cabinet that serves only to absorb as much of the backwave as possible. But this is clumsy and inefficient. In the 1950s, Edgar Villchur perfected a significant advance in the design of sealed-box loudspeakers. He put a highly compliant woofer with a heavy cone capable of long excursions (or *throw*) in a modestly sized sealed box. Because the cone moved relatively large distances in the cabinet, the trapped air acted as a spring, providing most of the restoring force that would be supplied by a stiff edge suspension on a woofer in an infinite-baffle enclosure. (The restoring force is what tends to keep the woofer cone centered when no signal is applied.)

This *acoustic-suspension* technique has a number of significant advantages. Because the air spring is very linear compared to a typical mechanical suspension, distortion tends to be low. And though the stiffness of the air in the box raises the woofer's resonance frequency (and therefore its low-frequency cutoff), the heavy cone with its floppy suspension has such a low resonance outside the box that it still can manage flat response down to 50 Hz or so in a relatively compact cabinet.

The main drawback of a classic acoustic-suspension design is low efficiency. The backwave is still essentially thrown away (a 3-dB loss right there), and the heavy cone requires more power to move than would a lighter diaphragm. Consequently, few modern sealed-box systems are pure acoustic-suspension loudspeakers. Most use lighter cones and depend partly on their edge suspensions for their restoring force.

Vented Enclosures

Another way of gaining efficiency is to use the backwave instead of just absorbing it. This is the idea behind bass-reflex loudspeakers. A *reflex speaker* incorporates a hole in its cabinet, called a *port,* whose resonance is tuned (usually with the aid of a tubular duct) to a frequency slightly below the resonance of the woofer itself. This frequency is carefully chosen to assure that the path traveled by the sound from the rear of the woofer is just long enough to put it in phase with the sound from the front when it emerges from the port, so that the two outputs reinforce, instead of cancel, each other. The tuning of the port also discriminates against frequencies outside the narrow band where the wavelength is just right.

An important variation on the standard bass-reflex concept is the use of what is known as a *passive radiator,* or *drone cone,* in place of an open port. Although it usually looks like a second woofer, a passive radiator has no motor and is not connected to the amplifier. By adjusting the mass of the passive radiator, a designer can achieve enclosure tunings that would not be possible with a simple port, often permitting the use of a smaller cabinet.

Either way, the output from the port—or passive radiator—reinforces the output of the woofer in the range where the driver's natural response is just beginning to fall off. What otherwise would be wasted energy works to extend the speaker's bass response. There is a price, however. Once the low end of a reflex system begins to fade, it rolls off twice as fast as that of a comparable acoustic-suspension speaker. And though the design of ported systems is far more scientific and predictable than it once was, there still is more guesswork involved than there is in developing an acoustic-suspension model. Finally, because the exact balance of the various tuning parameters (box size, woofer size, and so on) is so critical in a reflex system, they are more likely to drift somewhat out of proper alignment with age, possibly changing the low-frequency balance slightly.

Horn Loudspeakers

The granddaddy of loudspeaker enclosures is the horn, which looks and acts something like a megaphone. In its throat is an ordinary dynamic driver, but the horn's carefully shaped flare enables the diaphragm to couple much more efficiently to the air than if it were radiating directly from the front of the enclosure. Thus, the horn's main claim to fame is its ability to play very loud on a small amount of power. Unfortunately, a very large horn is needed to reproduce deep bass, so the technique is used mainly for midrange and treble drivers or for public-address applications in which low frequencies are not very important.

The Three Main Types of Loudspeaker Enclosures

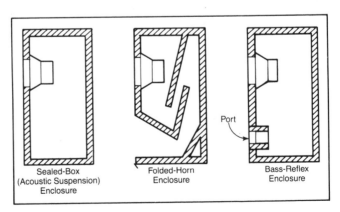

Sealed-Box (Acoustic Suspension) Enclosure

Folded-Horn Enclosure

Port

Bass-Reflex Enclosure

Cabinet Vibration

So much for the things an enclosure can do to help the sound. A poorly built cabinet also can make trouble by resonating and reradiating energy that it should absorb and dissipate internally. One reason speaker enclosures are almost always made of particleboard instead of birch or oak or some other "real" wood is that compressed sawdust has better internal damping than lumber. Most cabinets also have internal braces strategically located to minimize panel vibration. Other common resonance-control measures include use of extra-thick cabinet walls and application of damping materials.

In some high-end loudspeakers, the manufacturer goes a step further, using the drivers themselves to cancel the forces that tend to excite cabinet vibrations. For example, two woofers may be mounted on opposite sides of an enclosure with a rigid metal bar running between the backs of their baskets inside the speaker. If both are driven by the same signal, they will move in opposite directions so that mechanical energy that ordinarily would be transmitted to the cabinet is instead canceled in the bar linking the drivers.

Radiation Pattern

A loudspeaker's sound is determined primarily by its frequency response and its radiation pattern (sometimes called its *polar pattern*). What exactly constitutes the frequency response of a speaker is a tricky question. Is it the response only of the sound direct from the loudspeaker, or should reflected energy from the walls, floor, and ceiling be included as well? At any rate, it is generally accepted that the response, however one might measure it, should be reasonably flat at least from the bass through the lower treble and that it should remain smooth and fairly constant in all the directions in which the speaker radiates sound.

No such consensus exists for radiation pattern, which is one reason loudspeakers are so extremely varied in design. The most popular is the type produced by a conventional *front-firing box* loudspeaker. Very low frequencies, whose wavelengths are large relative to the baffle, spread out in all directions (omnidirectionally), while higher frequencies radiate mainly into the front hemisphere.

Next most common is a pattern that is *omnidirectional* at all frequencies. This tends to make the stereo image less precise but more spacious than is typical of front-firing speakers.

The third important category is *dipole* (sometimes called *doublet* or *figure-eight*) radiation. This pattern is typical of large panel speakers—most electrostatics, for example—whose driver diaphragms are exposed on both sides. Output to the sides is attenuated by cancella-

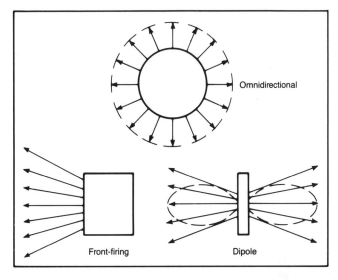

Three Main Loudspeaker Radiation Patterns. In practice, things are usually a little more complicated. Radiation pattern normally varies somewhat with frequency (front-firing loudspeakers are omnidirectional at very low frequencies, for example).

tion, and at very low frequencies, where the panel is too narrow to prevent sound waves from wrapping completely around, cancellation tends to occur in all directions, rolling off the deep bass. Speakers of this type can combine precise stereo localization with an unusually good sense of depth, but they can sound a little thin if they are not placed carefully to minimize low-frequency losses.

A final, somewhat wide-ranging, class of speakers comprises those whose radiation patterns are deliberately shaped to achieve some particular goal, such as a stable stereo image over a wide listening area or a big sound without undue loss of image precision. The latter, for example, might be achieved by placing drivers for some frequency ranges on both the front and back of the cabinet, to increase the amount of reflected sound.

Many people have strong preferences for one type or another of radiation pattern, but don't let anyone buffalo you into thinking that one is absolutely right and the others are completely wrong. It's not that simple. Listen and make up your mind about what's right for you.

Evaluating Loudspeakers

Having now been told repeatedly that you should choose speakers by listening to them, you may be wondering exactly what you should listen for. There are three main things: *tonal balance, bass extension,* and *stereo imaging.* But first lets talk about *how* you should listen and what you should do to prepare yourself.

Begin by thinking about how and where the speakers will be used. Listening to a bunch of floor-standing models makes no sense if you must put your loudspeakers on a shelf, for example. And if the speakers are to be used in a surround-sound system, what function will they perform? Ideally, all of the speakers in such a system should have a fairly similar tonal balance, at least through the midrange, but this is much more critical for the three front speakers (left, right, and center) than for the surround speakers, which can be of somewhat less distinguished pedigree without compromising the surround effect. In particular, the surround speakers can be relatively small, since Dolby Surround doesn't send much deep-bass information to the back.

When you're ready to visit a store, don't go empty-handed. Take some records or, better, Compact Discs that contain a variety of familiar music (and spend some time auditioning them through your present speakers, to help get your ears oriented). It's only natural that you're going to concentrate on music that you especially like, but even if your taste runs exclusively to rock, make sure that your choices include a good selection of acoustic instruments and both male and female vocals. (The ear is especially sensitive to errors in the reproduction of human voices.) The timbre of electronic instruments is too malleable to be a completely reliable guide to loudspeaker quality.

When you're listening, make sure that the speakers you're comparing are placed where their manufacturers recommend, or at least that if they are of similar design, they are not placed in such a way that one has an unfair advantage over the other. For example, putting a speaker near a room boundary, such as a wall or the floor, will enhance its low-frequency output; the more boundaries it is near, the more bass it will seem to have. So a loudspeaker will sound considerably different on a shelf near the middle of a wall than it will if moved down to the floor.

It also is important that you be able to make instantaneous A/B comparisons between models (don't try to do more than two at a time) with their volumes matched as closely as possible. The ear's frequency response is level-dependent, so even very small changes in volume affect our perception of tonal balance. In a listening comparison where levels aren't matched, the louder speaker will come off better than it would in a fair fight.

And don't let anyone rush you.

Tonal Balance

What strikes most people first about the sound of a loudspeaker is its tonal balance—the relative weight it gives to different parts of the audio spectrum. A good speaker will not favor any range of frequencies over the others. Be suspicious of a model that seems to have really impressive bass or a brilliant, up-front quality. When something jumps out at you like that, it often is a clue that the speaker is exaggerating instead of just reproducing. Also listen for smoothness, clarity, and

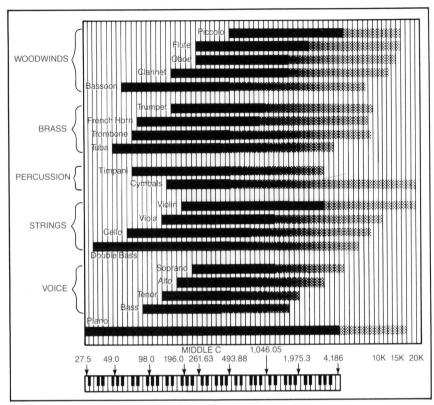

Frequency Ranges of Musical Instruments. The solid portions of the bars represent fundamentals, whereas the shaded parts are overtones. Note that few instruments produce any tones below about 50 Hz and that none of them generate fundamentals higher than about 5 kHz. Even the highest overtones seldom reach beyond 15 kHz.

freedom from harshness or distortion. High notes should be clean and appropriately bright, but not piercing or shrill; lows should be full, but not boomy or indistinct.

When you've got a feel for the overall balance, start probing how far down the speaker can go. Organ recordings often are good for this purpose. Really deep bass, below 40 Hz or so, is felt as much as it is heard, and it does not come along very often. A major reason that most of us are satisfied with speakers that are flat down to only 50 Hz or so is that very little music contains any energy at all below that frequency. But when there is something down there, it's nice to get a taste of it!

Do not expect miracles, however. A loudspeaker designer faces unavoidable compromises between size, efficiency, and bass extension. Reducing the volume of a speaker's enclosure forces a loss of efficiency, a curtailment of low-frequency response, or both. For this reason, a very small speaker will always sound a little deficient on the bottom compared to a significantly larger one.

Fortunately, there is one way out if you insist on good deep-bass response but won't abide a pair of big boxes in your living room: a *subwoofer*. This is a loudspeaker devoted strictly to reproducing low frequencies. Although a subwoofer that goes really low will be fairly large itself, you can get by with only one for both channels (your ears will use higher frequencies to establish the stereo image) and put it just about anywhere. Nowadays, some speaker systems are designed this way, with a pair of small speakers for the mids and highs and a third woofer module to handle the lows.

Finally, listen carefully to the stereo image presented by a pair of speakers. How well are instruments localized, and how stable are their apparent positions? Voices and instruments should not sound as though they are wandering around, unless this is a purposeful effect in the recording. Nor should they sound oversized or excessively diffuse. On the other hand, there's no need to become obsessive about pinpoint imaging unless you just happen to prefer it. Although extremely tight, specific localization of voices and instruments often is spoken of as though it were the only respectable goal, many people prefer a bigger, more open sound and a somewhat less precise rendering of the stereo stage. It's very much a matter of taste (which pretty well sums up the entire process of selecting loudspeakers).

Loudspeaker Specifications

Impedance
The load a speaker presents to the amplifier driving it. Although specified as a single value, loudspeaker impedances normally vary widely with frequency. Ratings are almost always between 4 and 8 ohms, which is a good range for modern amplifiers and receivers, and they typically (though not always) represent something close to the speaker's minimum impedance. The exact figure is not critical.

Sensitivity
How loud a speaker can play for a given signal level. The standard rating is the sound pressure level (SPL), in decibels, at a distance of one meter for an input of 2.8 volts (equivalent to 1 watt into 8 ohms). Sensitivities of most modern speakers hover in the vicinity of 90 dB. A rating of 86 dB would be quite low, whereas one of 94 dB would be unusually high. Although a high sensitivity is not inherently better than a low one, it can save you money on your amp or receiver. A 3-dB increase in speaker sensitivity will halve your power requirements.

Minimum Power
The amount of power the manufacturer thinks your amp or receiv-

er must be capable of providing for the speaker to perform satisfactorily. There is no standard way of arriving at this rating, so it is not useful for making comparisons between speakers from different manufacturers.

Maximum Power

Again, there is no standard, so ratings from different manufacturers are not comparable. Equally meaningless (for the same reason), but more misleading. Most people think that they will damage their speakers if they attach them to amplifiers with power ratings that exceed the speakers' rated maxima. Unless you run your speakers at abusive volumes, a big amplifier is scarcely more dangerous to them than a small one. Don't worry, be happy.

Frequency Response

As we've already noted, a speaker's frequency response depends significantly on how it is measured, which reduces its value as an index of quality. A typical specification might read "55 Hz to 20 kHz, ±3 dB"—pretty good for a loudspeaker. Specifications that give only a frequency range, such as 20 Hz to 20 kHz, without a tolerance are worthless and should be ignored.

Distortion

You may sometimes see a distortion specification for a loudspeaker—perhaps even a plot of distortion versus frequency for various drive levels. Speakers produce much more distortion than electronic components, such as receivers. Figures of 0.5 percent or so at middle and high frequencies are not uncommon at moderate volume, and distortion usually will rise to several percent at very low frequencies (below 100 Hz) and at high output levels.

Chapter 4

Turntables and Phono Cartridges

Turntables and Phono Cartridges

If you don't already own phonograph records and can get whatever music you want on Compact Disc, there's not much reason to invest in record-playing equipment. But if you have a substantial collection of LPs, as most of us still do, you doubtless want to make them sound their best. In that case, now is probably a better time to buy than later, since the variety of record-playing equipment available is shrinking year by year.

A turntable has four basic parts: a platter approximately twelve inches across that holds the record, a motor to turn the platter, a tonearm to hold a phono cartridge, or pickup, in correct relation to the record being played, and a base to hold these parts together and isolate them from external vibration. Ideally, it should do nothing more. The platter should turn at the correct speed, with no variation, and it should transmit no vibration from the motor or the environment through the record to the stylus ("needle") of the phono cartridge. The

A Turntable

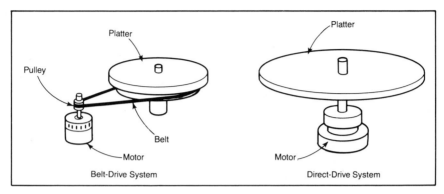

Platter

Platter

Pulley

Belt

Motor

Motor

Belt-Drive System

Direct-Drive System

Turntable Drive Systems

tonearm should exert enough downward force on the cartridge to keep the stylus securely in the record groove, but it also should move freely in whatever direction the stylus carries it.

Belt-Drive vs. Direct-Drive

Clearly, a great deal depends on the drive mechanism for the platter. Two techniques are now used for high-fidelity turntables: belt-drive and direct-drive. In a belt-drive turntable, the platter is connected to the motor by an elastic belt, which minimizes transmission of vibration from the motor to the record. The platter itself usually is fairly heavy, with most of the mass concentrated near its edge, creating a flywheel effect to even out any short-term variations in the motor speed. Not so long ago, belt-drive was unquestionably the best way to go for a high-quality home turntable, and many excellent models continue to use it. But the development of high-performance direct-drive turntables has given belt-drive a worthy competitor at the top of the turntable market and a sound thrashing in the middle of the market, where most high-fidelity equipment is sold.

In a direct-drive turntable, the shaft of a low-speed motor attaches directly to the platter spindle. This arrangement puts a premium on the quality of the motor. It must turn very smoothly and with exceedingly little vibration. But when these goals are met, the results can be exceptionally good. Most direct-drive turntables use electronic servo speed-control systems to lock the drive motor to an extremely precise quartz-crystal oscillator, assuring correct speed with minimal variation.

Manual vs. Automatic

Turntables also are distinguished by the degree to which they automate the process of playing records. Models that sift unattended through an entire stack of LPs have fallen out of favor and now are quite rare, but most will put the stylus down on the disc for you, pick up the tonearm at the end of the side, return it to rest, and then shut off the motor. These are called *automatic* turntables. *Semiautomatic* units expect you to lower the stylus onto the record. However, they will at least pick it up at the end, and some will return the arm and automatically shut off as well. A few, mostly very high-end, turntables are completely passive: They play the records; you do everything else. Some even come without a tonearm, so you are required (or enabled, depending on your point of view) to buy one separately.

Although the clumsy mechanics of early automatic turntables were good reason to avoid them, the choice now is strictly one of personal preference. Automation no longer exacts a price in performance.

The Suspension

Like a car, a turntable needs shock absorbers to isolate it from external jolts and vibration. Disturbing influences can range from footsteps on the floor to the music itself, which may be picked up by the turntable base, passed on to the stylus and from there back through the amplifier and speakers, creating a vicious circle know as *acoustic feedback,* or, more evocatively, *howlback.*

The best defense against acoustic feedback is what's called a *sprung-subchassis suspension.* The tonearm and platter are mounted on a rigid frame or plate that is isolated from the base by soft springs. By careful choice of subchassis mass and spring compliance, it is possible to move the resonance frequency of the assembly down very low—preferably to just a few hertz. This makes the turntable very insensitive to acoustic feedback. Unfortunately, unless the springs are damped in some way (which can reduce the suspension's effectiveness against feedback), this type of suspension may overreact to disturbances at extremely low frequencies, such as footfalls or vibration from truck traffic.

More commonly, the tonearm and platter are mounted directly to the base, which rests on a set of feet designed to damp out vibration. The virtues and drawbacks of this kind of suspension are a mirror image of those for a sprung-subchassis design. Resistance to ultralow-frequency vibration usually is better, but rejection of acoustic feedback is worse. However, the latter can be minimized by the use of materials with good internal damping in the construction of the base (high-density particle board, for example).

The Tonearm

A tonearm usually is a long, slender metal tube attached near the back

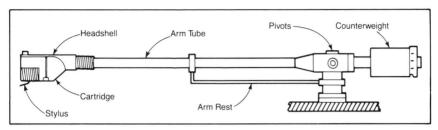

Side View of a Tonearm

to a low-friction pivot assembly that enables it to move freely up and down and from side to side. At the front is a platform, called a *headshell,* to which the cartridge attaches. (Sometimes the headshell is removable, to simplify installation or exchange of pickups.) Behind the pivot is a heavy cylindrical counterweight that can be moved back and forth slightly to balance the weight of the front of the arm and the cartridge.

On most tonearms, the counterweight is moved a little forward of the position that would give perfect balance in order to apply the necessary downward force of the stylus against the record groove. These are *static-balance* designs. A *dynamic-balance* arm applies the downforce with a calibrated spring. Dynamic balance has the advantage of not requiring that the turntable be level for proper operation. On the other hand, the characteristics of the spring may change with age, throwing off the accuracy of its calibration.

Modern pivoted tonearms also include an adjustment for anti-skating compensation—a force applied laterally to counteract the arm's tendency to pull toward the center of the record, causing uneven pressure on the groove walls. This effect is caused by the geometry of pivoted arms, which angles the headshell toward the inside of the record to keep it as nearly tangent to the groove as possible over as much of the record as possible. The better this alignment is maintained, the lower the distortion produced by the cartridge will be.

Linear-Tracking Tonearms

Theoretically, a better kind of tonearm would be one that moved the cartridge in a straight line across the record, keeping the stylus constantly tangent to the groove. Early attempts at this worked rather poorly because of excessive friction and other problems. These difficulties have since been eliminated, making linear-tracking (or straight-line tracking) turntables practical. They are, however, more complex mechanically and therefore at somewhat greater risk of breakdown. And the performance improvement is, practically speaking, rather modest.

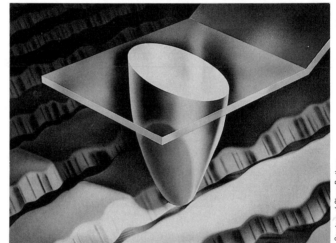

Mono and Stereo Record Grooves.
The grooves of a mono record are laterally cut with the same information on both walls. On a stereo record, the grooves are cut both laterally and vertically, enabling the inner and outer walls to carry different information for the left and right channels.

Mono Record Groove

Stereo Record Groove

Stylus in a Groove.
The stylus follows the tiny undulations in the groove walls. Its motions are transmitted by the cantilever tube to the cartridge body, where they are converted to an electrical signal.

Phono Cartridges

When you look closely at how records are made and reproduced, it's hard to believe the system actually works. All of the music is represented as tiny wiggles molded into the walls of the spiral groove that runs from the outer edge to the label of the disc. The higher the frequency, the more tightly packed they are; the louder the sound, the bigger the wiggle. The groove walls open out at an angle of approximately 45 degrees. On a mono record, the two walls are cut identically, but on a stereo disc, one wall carries the left channel and the other, the right.

This information is picked up by a minuscule stylus, usually made of carefully ground and polished diamond, attached to a slender cantilever. (The cantilever most often is an aluminum tube, but other materials sometimes are used instead.) It is secured to the cartridge body near one end by a block of rubberlike material so that it is still free to vibrate. The stylus traces along the recorded spiral, moving the cantilever in response to the groove modulation.

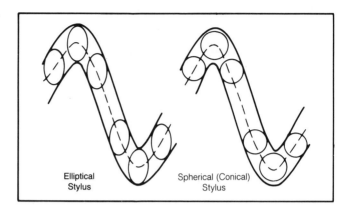

Elliptical
Stylus

Spherical (Conical)
Stylus

Moving-Magnet and Moving-Coil

The details of what happens inside the cartridge body vary according to the exact design, but in high-fidelity pickups, the basic principle usually is magnetic. The most common approach is called the *moving-magnet* technique. In this type of pickup, a tiny, powerful, permanent magnet is attached to the end of the cantilever that protrudes from the mounting block into the cartridge body. It is situated between a set of wire coils wound around iron cores, or pole pieces. The coils are mounted at 45-degree angles, corresponding to the angles of the walls of a record groove. The motion of the magnet's field through the windings of the coils induces currents in them proportional to the velocity of the stylus in the groove. (The pole pieces increase the efficiency of the magnetic induction, thereby increasing the output voltage.) These are the signals that pass through the wires leading from the tonearm to your amplifier or receiver.

Another fairly popular type of cartridge is the *moving-coil,* in which the usual relationship of magnet and coils is reversed: The magnet is fixed, and the coils are attached to the cantilever. Unfortunately, the coils must be made quite small to keep their mass down, which usually results in much lower output than is produced by moving-magnet models. This increases susceptibility to hum and forces the use of a step-up transformer or an additional stage of amplification. Many amplifiers and receivers now have phono inputs that can be switched to handle either type of cartridge.

Despite significant advances in the design of moving-coil cartridges, it is much easier to build a good moving-magnet, and most of the best pickups are of this variety. The one consistent advantage of moving-coils is that they have very low output impedances and therefore perform essentially the same with a wide range of phono-input impedances. Moving-magnet cartridges, on the other hand, typically require a load of approximately 47,000 ohms in parallel with some fairly specific capacitance. Modern designs are less finicky about loading than was common in the past, but you can still expect some high-frequency response error if the combined capacitance of the tonearm leads and the phono input is too far off the mark.

Stylus Shapes

The grooves in a record master (from which the stampers used to press discs are made) are cut by a heated, wedge-shaped head. For lowest distortion in playback, the pickup stylus should approximate that shape as accurately as is practical. On the other hand, it can't come too close, or it may actually recut the groove in the record as it passes through.

In the beginning, all cartridges had what is known as a spherical, or conical, stylus because that shape was easy to make. Unfortunately, the wide contact area of such a stylus has trouble following the tight turns of a high-frequency groove modulation. For this reason, most high-fidelity cartridges now use what is known as an elliptical stylus, which makes the contact area taller and narrower. Elliptical styli trace high frequencies better than spherical styli, thereby reducing distortion.

The very best cartridges now use what are called *multiradial,* or *line-contact,* styli, which further heighten and narrow the contact patch. The earliest such stylus was the Shibata, originally developed for playback of CD-4 discrete quadraphonic records, but many other variations have been introduced since then. Alignment of these styli is more critical than it is for the other types, but when they are set up correctly, they trace high frequencies even better than ellipticals. At the same time, they distribute the tracking force over a greater total area, so that pressure on the groove walls and consequent wear are diminished.

The pressure at the area of contact between stylus and groove is surprisingly large—so great that even diamond styli eventually start to wear down, increasing distortion and impairing tracking. When that starts to happen, you need a new stylus assembly, which on most pickups can simply be slipped into place. Typically, you can get somewhere between five hundred and one thousand hours of service from a stylus, so figure on a replacement every one to three years, depending on how much you listen to records.

Arm/Cartridge Matching

A seldom-mentioned but important factor in the performance of a

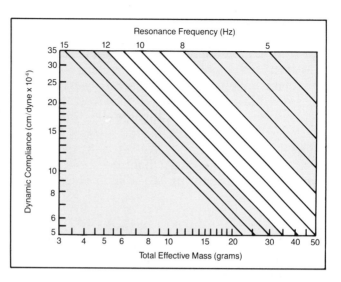

Tonearm/Cartridge Matching Graph. For best performance, the low-frequency arm/cartridge resonance should fall between approximately 8 and 12 Hz—low enough not to affect frequency response in the audio band but not so far down that the system gets overstimulated by record warps. This graph shows the relationship between resonance frequency, the low-frequency dynamic compliance of the cartridge, and the effective moving mass of the arm/cartridge combination.

record-playing system is the low-frequency resonance established by the effective moving mass of the tonearm and cartridge and the compliance of the stylus cantilever suspension. It is like the classic example of a weight on a spring. If you hold the end of the spring and move your hand up and down slowly, everything will tend to move together as a unit, and there will be little relative motion between your hand and the weight. If you gradually increase the frequency of your hand movements, the weight eventually will start to bob up and down. Soon after that, you will reach a frequency at which the weight moves a very large amount for small movements of your hand. This is the *resonance,* or natural, frequency of the weighted spring, where the transfer of energy from your hand to the spring-suspended weight is extremely efficient. As the speed of your hand's movement continues to increase and passes the resonance frequency, the weight's motion will diminish again until it is nearly stationary, with the spring coiling and uncoiling above it. The resonance frequency will increase if the weight's mass is reduced or the spring is stiffened; it will decrease if the weight is made greater or the compliance of the spring is increased.

At the arm/cartridge resonance frequency, there will be a large hump in the response, because any excitation at that frequency will cause an exaggerated movement of the stylus relative to the tonearm. Consequently, the resonance is best kept below the audio band. On the other hand, if it is too low, it will land in the frequency range occupied by most record warps, below about 5 Hz. So, the resonance should fall between 7 and 15 Hz—preferably, between 8 and 12 Hz.

You can calculate the frequency of the arm/cartridge resonance if you know the effective mass of the tonearm (not the same as its weight of total mass), the weight of the pickup (to be added to the effective mass of the arm), and the dynamic compliance of the cartridge at very low frequencies. In fact, we have provided a graph that shows the relationship. Unfortunately, reliable figures for effective tonearm mass and cartridge compliance are very hard to come by. Your best bet on this one is an empirical approach. Observe the cartridge stylus from the side while playing a record that looks flat (it will still have a lot of small warps). If the stylus appears steady and moves as a unit with the cartridge body and tonearm, you're okay. But if the stylus appears to be bobbing up and down, the resonance is too low. In that case, you need a lighter tonearm, a lighter or lower-compliance cartridge, or some means of damping the system to reduce the amplitude of the resonance.

P-Mount Arms and Cartridges

The most convenient solution to the resonance problem, along with a number of others, is the P-Mount system. At first glance, it appears to be just a simplified, plug-in method of mounting a cartridge—in itself a big advance over the standard method, which requires that you fiddle with tiny wires and screws. But P-Mount defines many physical characteristics of the arm and cartridge, so that when you plug in a cartridge, the low-frequency resonance will be in the proper range, the stylus will be aligned to the groove for minimum distortion, and the tracking force will be correctly set. It takes virtually all of the fuss and bother out of cartridge installation while assuring the best performance of which the combination is capable.

Turntable Specifications

Speed Accuracy
The platter's rotational speed should, at worst, be within about 1 percent of the correct value, and ½ percent is a more reasonable standard. For example, it might be stated as 33⅓ RPM, ±0.5%. Most modern turntables, especially those with electronic speed control, do better than that.

Wow and Flutter
These are very short-term speed variations caused by inevitable imperfections in turntable bearings and motors. *Wow,* which comprises slow variations, is heard as pitch instability—a sourness on sustained tones. It is especially noticeable on held piano notes. (Most audible wow results not from inadequate turntable mechanisms, but from records with off-center spindle holes or warps.) *Flutter* consists of higher-frequency variations and usually is heard as a coarsening of the sound.

The specification for wow and flutter will depend on the method used to measure it. Best is the IEEE/ANSI standard technique, but most common is the looser WRMS (JIS) method. (*WRMS* stands for *weighted RMS*.) In any event, you should expect to see figures of less than 0.1 percent for acceptability and less than 0.05 percent for premium equipment.

Rumble
Low-frequency noise caused by motor vibration. Like any other signal-to-noise (S/N) ratio, rumble should be weighted to reflect the ear's reduced sensitivity at the frequency extremes. Probably the best weighting technique for rumble is the ARLL (audible rumble loudness level) method, but the most common is the more forgiving DIN B curve. Audible rumble is rare on modern component-grade turntables, and you should see specifications of -60 dB or less.

Cartridge Specifications

Frequency Response
Response should extend smoothly from 20 Hz to 20 kHz, remaining within $\pm 1\frac{1}{2}$ dB or less from 30 Hz to 15 kHz. The largest variations usually are at high frequencies.

Channel Separation
Separation should be at least 20 dB at midband (around 1 kHz).

Channel Balance
Output from the two channels should be nearly the same for identical groove modulations, or else the stereo image will be shifted to the stronger side. They should be within ± 1 dB (2 dB total) or less of each other.

Sensitivity (Output Voltage)
The output for a given peak lateral stylus velocity. Ratings between 0.5 and 1.0 millivolts per centimeter per second (mV/cm/sec) are typical for moving-magnet pickups, and some high-output moving-coils approach the lower end of that range. More often, the specification is given in terms of output for a stylus velocity of 5 cm/sec, making the typical ratings 2.5-5.0 millivolts. The sensitivity of a low-output moving-coil cartridge usually will be only 5-10 percent that of a moving-magnet.

Load Impedance
The resistance and parallel capacitance to which the cartridge

should be attached for flattest frequency response. (The resistive part of the load is contributed by your amplifier or receiver's phono input; the capacitive portion comes from both the phono input and the tonearm cables.) For moving-magnet cartridges, a resistive load of 47,000 ohms is standard, and anything within about 3,000 ohms up or down should be okay. Optimum capacitance varies according to the design of the pickup, but it usually is between 100 and 500 picofarads (pF). In general, cartridges are not as finicky about this as they used to be, but it still is a good idea to get the capacitance within 100 pF of what the manufacturer recommends. Loading for moving-coil cartridges is usually noncritical unless a step-up transformer is used.

Vertical Tracking Angle (VTA)
The angle between the record surface and a line extending between the contact point of the stylus in the groove and the pivot point in the cantilever mounting block. Theoretically, the VTA should be close to the standard of 20 degrees for minimum distortion. In practice, however, the optimum value is difficult to determine precisely and does not appear to be critical.

Vertical Tracking Force (VTF)
The downward force on the stylus required for proper tracking of the groove without excessive wear. (Curiously, this specification traditionally has been given in grams—a unit of mass—rather than in a true unit of force, such as dynes or millinewtons.) Some low-compliance moving-coil cartridges require tracking forces in the range of 2-2½ grams, which is rather high. More typical figures would be 1-1¼ grams. It usually is best to run a cartridge near the high side of its recommended tracking-force range, since mistracking will cause more groove damage than will a slightly higher constant pressure.

Tracking Ability
The ability of the stylus to maintain contact with the groove at high modulation velocities. Mistracking causes severe distortion and groove damage, so this is an important characteristic. Tracking ability is seldom specified, however, and there is no standard way of measuring it. Fortunately, it is easy to assess by listening. High frequencies tend to cause the most trouble, so records with blaring trumpets or powerfully struck high notes on a piano are good tools. Listen for bursts of harshness or sibilance, indicating momentary mistracking. Just remember during your evaluations that mistracking may damage a record at the point where it occurs to such an extent that the disc will forever after sound distorted

there, even when properly tracked. Most manufacturers' top models track very well, especially the moving-magnet designs.

Distortion

Cartridge distortion depends on many factors, including stylus velocity, stylus shape, and orientation of the stylus to the groove. It tends to be high by the standards of other components, although seldom great enough to be audible except at high stylus velocities. Manufacturers seldom list a distortion specification for their phono pickups.

Chapter 5

Tape Decks

Tape Decks

Magnetic tape has been music's great liberator—first by making practical the continuous recording of long, complex works and later by making these recordings completely portable. Tape is now by far the most popular medium for the enjoyment of recorded music.

The first magnetic recording system was invented in 1898 by Vlademar Poulsen. His "telegraphone" dictating machine used steel wire on a rotating cylinder and a moving recording head connected to a simple carbon microphone. Tape recording, as such, was developed in the thirties and has made great strides since.

How Magnetic Recording Works

Modern recording tape consists of a thin polyester film coated on one side with very fine particles of some metallic substance that can be magnetized. These particles are suspended in a binder that adheres tightly to the plastic backing material. In conventional analog (as opposed to digital) recording, the music signal is recorded as variations in the strength and polarity (north or south) of the magnetization of these particles, corresponding to the amplitude and polarity (positive or negative) of the input.

You can visualize the process by thinking of the particles as containing microscopic bar magnets, each with its own north and south magnetic poles. In raw tape, these magnets are randomly oriented so that the net magnetic field of the tape is virtually nil. A tape deck's recording head is essentially an electromagnet with its external field concentrated in the vicinity of a small gap in the head's metal pole piece. The pole piece has wire wrapped around it. This wire carries the input signal current, which induces an alternating magnetic field in the pole piece. The field emerges from the gap so that as the tape slides across the head's surface, the magnetic field penetrates and magnetizes nearby particles in the tape coating.

The polarity of the current through the head winding (positive or

Tape Construction. Recording tape has two layers: a tough, plastic base film and a surface coating of magnetizable particles suspended in a binder that secures them to the base.

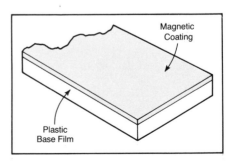

Magnetic Coating

Plastic Base Film

A Cassette Deck

negative) determines the polarity of the magnetic field in the gap; the amplitude of the current determines the strength of the field. The particles in the tape coating tend to align themselves magnetically with the field in the gap, so that their south poles face in the direction of what is, at that moment, the gap's north pole, and their north poles face in the direction of the gap's south pole. The stronger the input signal (and therefore the field in the gap), the more uniform the magnetic orientation of the tape particles. And, the greater the magnetic uniformity among the particles, the stronger the field retained by the tape.

Thus, the electrical properties of the input signal are mirrored in the magnetic characteristics of the recorded tape. All that is necessary to retrieve the original signal is to reverse the process. The tape is passed over a second head (or the same head, in cassette decks with combined record/play heads), and the variation of the magnetic field passing the gap induces a current in the head winding corresponding to the changes in the field strength and polarity, thereby reconstructing the recorded signal. It's almost as simple as that.

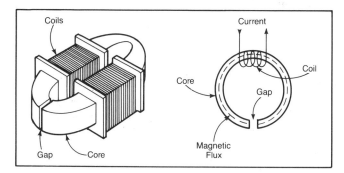

Tape-Head Construction. In recording, a tape head functions as a small electromagnet powered by the audio signal. The current flowing through its coils induces a magnetic field in the metal pole pieces they are wrapped around. A gap between the pole pieces enables the field to penetrate the tape effectively and alter its magnetic state. During playback, the system works in reverse, with the passing magnetic field of the tape picked up at the gap, inducing an electrical current in the coils.

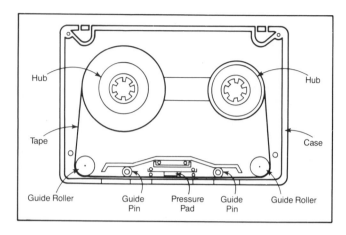

Open-Reel vs. Cassette

The first tape recorders used a pair of large spools, with the tape threaded from the supply reel through a head assembly to a take-up reel. This system still prevails today in recording studios and radio stations, where performance and ease of editing are more important than size or convenience. But in the consumer market, recorders that use the Compact Cassette have almost completely replaced the bulky, expensive open-reel machines that once were king.

Essentially, a cassette is a small, encapsulated version of the open-reel tape path. Tiny supply and take-up hubs are housed in a plastic shell. The tape is preloaded, threading down from one hub, over a pair of pins that hold it flat across an opening on the bottom edge of the shell, and up to the other hub. When a cassette is inserted into a recorder, the hubs fit down over spindles that turn them, and the exposed section of tape is positioned right in front of the tape heads, which are pressed up against it during recording or playback.

The miniaturization of the cassette relative to open-reel tape is achieved by a couple of means. One is a reduction in tape width, from ¼ to ⅛ inch. The other is a reduction in tape speed, from a minimum of 3¾ ips (inches per second) on open-reel decks to 1⅞ ips on cassette decks. But, as usually is the case, you don't get something for nothing: A price is paid in performance. All else being equal, cassettes are noisier than open-reel tape and reach saturation (maximum magnetization) at lower signal levels, especially at high frequencies. Fortunately, manufacturers of cassette decks and tape have lavished an enormous amount of research and development on overcoming these limitations of the format, with gratifying results. Henceforward, we will be focusing our attention almost exclusively on cassette decks and tape, though some elements of the discussion apply to the open-reel format as well.

Tape Types

One line of attack has been the formulation of tape coatings designed specifically for use in cassettes. Early cassettes used tape that was very similar to open-reel formulations, but slit narrower. Their simple ferric-oxide coatings now would make them Type I tapes, according to the IEC (International Electrotechnical Commission) system of classification. Modern occupants of that category are much improved in every respect, however.

The first big breakthrough in cassette tape was the development of coatings using chromium dioxide (CrO_2) for the magnetic particles. Chrome's superior high-frequency performance and lower noise made it a natural for the new format. Since then, many tape makers have come up with cobalt-doped ferric-oxide formulations whose magnetic characteristics mimic those of chromium dioxide. Both are regarded as Type II tapes in the IEC classification scheme.

After a brief flirtation with dual-layer chrome and ferric coatings (the Type III ferrichromes), manufacturers turned their attention to creating pure-metal particles for use in place of oxides. Unfortunately, the finely ground metal powders needed for tape coatings are prone to explosive oxidation when exposed to air, so the development process was not an easy one. But the reward for eventual success was a significant increase in the maximum signal level that could be retained on a cassette without distortion. This is important when recording music that has a wide dynamic range—that is, a large difference between the loudest and softest levels. Although pure-metal particles have been adapted in a few cases to have Type II characteristics, most tapes made with them are classified as Type IV.

The introduction of Type II and IV tapes and the great improvement in Type I formulations over the years have significantly advanced the cassette's performance as a high-fidelity medium for music recording. But every enhancement involves an alteration in the magnetic properties of the tape. This, in turn, requires adjustments of certain operating characteristics of the deck. Two of these parameters—bias and equalization—are of fundamental importance.

Bias

Tape responds nonlinearly to weak fields, because of what you might think of as magnetic friction: It takes a certain amount of energy just to get the particles to begin any magnetic reorientation. This creates severe distortion at low signal levels. For that reason, all modern tape decks mix an ultrasonic tone, called *bias,* with the input signal, to keep the recording head's field strength up out of the tape's nonlinear region. (Bias is typically at frequencies around 100 kHz and is therefore completely inaudible apart from its effect on how the tape accepts the audio signal.)

The exact amount of bias required varies widely according to the tape formulation. In general, Type I tapes take the least amount of bias and Type IV, the most. Every high-fidelity cassette deck provides for switching the bias level to accommodate the various types of tape. But there are significant differences between tapes within a category, as well. Consequently, almost all tape decks have internal (sometimes external) bias trimmers for making the necessary adjustments. This is one reason it is important with most decks to follow the manufacturer's tape recommendations: The machines are preadjusted at the factory for the magnetic characteristics of certain tapes, and if the tape you use is too dissimilar, you will get poor recordings.

If too much bias is used, high-frequency response will be impaired, causing recordings to sound dull. But if too little bias is applied, the opposite will occur: High frequencies will be accentuated, leading to an overly bright or shrill sound. In addition, distortion will increase and the amount of signal the tape can accept at middle frequencies without overloading will decline.

Equalization

For various reasons, a signal recorded with flat frequency response will play back with rolloffs at low and high frequencies. Equalization (EQ) is used in both recording and playback to compensate for these losses and to reduce tape hiss somewhat. High frequencies are boosted in recording. During playback, the treble is cut by a smaller amount, which restores flat high-frequency response and reduces tape noise, and the low frequencies are boosted.

The amount of equalization used is specified with a *time constant.* Confused? Well, don't worry about it. All you really need to know is that smaller time constants correspond to larger treble cuts. The original standard for cassette playback equalization was 120 microseconds (120 μsec), which is still used for Type I tapes. (The *recording* equalization can be whatever the deck manufacturer needs to get flat response from a tape with the standard playback EQ.) But the enhanced high-frequency sensitivity and headroom of Type II tapes prompted the adoption of a new, more aggressive 70-μsec playback equalization. The result is an improvement of several decibels in signal-to-noise ratio. And when Type IV (metal) tapes were introduced, the 70-μsec EQ was adopted for them as well.

The two playback equalization curves are standardized and therefore the same for all recorders and tape formulations (theoretically, at least). But as with bias, the optimum recording EQ varies according to the exact performance characteristics of the deck and the tape.

Setting Bias and Equalization

All modern high-fidelity cassette decks provide some means for switching equalization during playback and both bias and EQ during recording to suit the tape type in use. This can be as simple as a switch with positions for "normal" (Type I), "chrome" (Type II), and "metal" (Type IV). Some decks will do this switching for you automatically, based on the presence or absence of notches in certain positions on the back edge of the cassette. A small minority enable you to select bias and equalization separately, but since it almost always is best to stick with the standard combinations of bias and EQ for a particular tape type, this elaboration is more a potential source of confusion than a useful feature.

As we mentioned earlier, however, the magnetic characteristics of tapes vary considerably even within a type. For example, one manufacturer's premium Type II formulation may give very flat frequency response on a particular deck, while another company's top Type II might have a rising high-frequency response in the same machine. One way of dealing with this problem is to use only the tapes recommended by the manufacturer of your cassette deck. But since tape makers are constantly improving their products—changing their magnetic characteristics in the process—this approach will eventually prove inadequate.

Fortunately, many cassette decks provide some means of dealing with these variations. The simplest is a front-panel bias adjustment. This is just a knob that enables you to increase or decrease the bias until you reach a setting that gives the best frequency response for the tape you are using. Unfortunately, finding the correct setting by ear can be a tedious undertaking. Next up the ladder are decks with internal test-tone generators that can be used together with the recording-level meters to make the adjustment quick and precise. The most sophisticated adjustment systems use on-board microcomputers to automatically calibrate both bias and recording equalization for lowest distortion and flattest response.

Dolby Noise Reduction

Originally developed for dictation machines, the cassette was at first an unpromising medium for high-fidelity music recording. Topping the list of problems was noise. Narrow tape and slow transport speed make it difficult to achieve an adequate signal-to-noise ratio. The big breakthrough was the development of Dolby B noise-reduction, a consumer rendition of the Dolby A system that already had revolutionized professional recording. Dolby B is a stripped-down version of its progenitor, designed to significantly diminish the most audible noise with a minimum of electronic complexity. Consequently, it operates

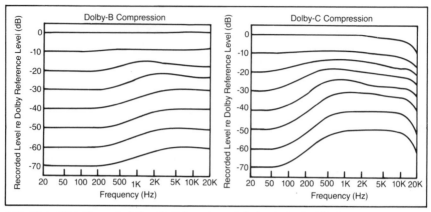

Dolby Recording Characteristics. The Dolby system works by boosting low-level high-frequency signals during recording and reducing them (along with tape hiss) by the same amount during playback. Shown here are the Dolby B and C recording curves for various signal levels. Note that Dolby C applies greater boost over a wider frequency range than does Dolby B, yielding greater noise reduction on playback.

mainly at high frequencies instead of in multiple bands covering the entire audio range as Dolby A does. Nonetheless, it is a very sophisticated system that can sharply attenuate tape hiss without changing the sound in any other way.

Dolby noise-reduction is a double-ended, or encode/decode, type of system. During recording, low-level high-frequency signals are boosted to keep them relatively strong when they go on the tape. In playback, this process is exactly reversed, attenuating high frequencies just enough to restore flat frequency response. But since tape hiss comes off the tape at an essentially constant level and the Dolby decoder reduces it along with the treble portion of the signal, the level of the signal relative to that of the hiss (that is, the signal-to-noise ratio) is better than it would have been without the Dolby processing.

The amount of treble boost the Dolby encoder applies during recording varies according to the amount of high-frequency energy in

Effectiveness of Dolby Noise Reduction. These plots of noise level versus frequency demonstrate the hiss reduction afforded by the Dolby B and C systems.

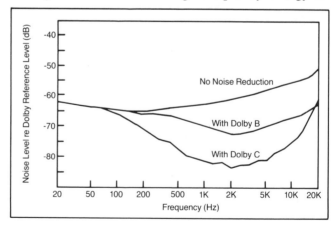

the signal. As the signal level in the range affected by the Dolby process decreases, the amount of boost increases, until the signal drops below a certain threshold. From that point down, the amount of boost remains constant. This prevents any audible variation in the amount of background noise during playback—a very annoying phenomenon known as "hiss pumping"—and is one of the keys to the Dolby system's unobtrusive effectiveness as a noise-reducer.

Dolby B improves the signal-to-noise ratio of a tape deck by approximately ten decibels, which is enough to assure clean, quiet recordings of most music—but not all. To handle music with extremely wide dynamic range (increasingly common since the advent of the digital Compact Disc), Dolby Laboratories developed an enhanced consumer noise-reduction system called *Dolby C*. It expands the range of frequencies covered and increases the maximum boost applied during recording, nearly doubling the amount of noise reduction, while reducing the amount of boost applied at very high frequencies, to prevent tape overload and thereby improve response in the extreme treble. Nearly all high-fidelity cassette decks for the home now include both Dolby B and C noise reduction.

Dolby Drawbacks

On a properly adjusted deck, Dolby is an almost-perfect noise-reduction system, attenuating hiss with no audible side effects. But if a tape machine has significant response errors at high frequencies (because of an incorrect bias setting, for example) or if the Dolby circuits themselves are miscalibrated, there will be problems. Dolby processing tends to exaggerate response errors within the band over which it operates. So if a deck's response without noise reduction rises at high frequencies, it will rise more when Dolby is used; and if the response rolls off in the treble, it will roll off more with Dolby. And since Dolby C's action is stronger than Dolby B's, it also is more sensitive to response errors.

This response sensitivity is usually most troublesome when playing back a tape on a deck other than the one on which it was made. If the perpendicularity of the playback head to the tape (the *playback azimuth*) doesn't exactly match that of the head used to record the tape (the *recording azimuth*), there will be high-frequency losses. Azimuth alignment between the recording and playback heads on a deck almost always is excellent, but azimuth discrepancies *between* decks are common and sometimes severe.

The other source of error in Dolby processing arises from its level-dependency. Because Dolby noise-reduction boosts high frequencies more at low levels than at high levels, the decoding circuitry must "know" how much cut to apply for any given signal level and frequency that comes off the tape in playback. Otherwise, it may cut too little or too much, thereby introducing a response error. Unfortunately, tape formulations vary in their sensitivity, which means that for the same input, one will have more output than another. Consequently, the Dolby encoder must be calibrated to tape sensitivity to ensure that the decoder (whose characteristics are fixed) will behave appropriately on playback.

Cassette decks come from the factory with preset Dolby calibrations for a certain tape of each type (I, II, and IV), which is fine as long as you stick with those tapes. Otherwise, you will need to readjust the Dolby calibration to assure optimum performance. Most decks that provide test tones for bias adjustment also supply another tone generator that can be used with the deck's meters to recalibrate the Dolby encoder. And the handful of decks that can automatically adjust bias and equalization normally provide the same service for Dolby-encoder calibration in the process.

Again, Dolby C is more finicky than Dolby B, and though it is almost as universal as Dolby B on home decks, many car and portable tape players include only B. (You can play back a C-encoded tape through a Dolby-B decoder, just as you can play a Dolby-B tape back with no decoding at all, but the sound will be overbright and the noise-reduction effect will be partially lost.) In general, it is a good idea to stick with Dolby B unless you simply can't get a quiet enough recording without moving up to C. This is especially important for tapes that you expect to play back on machines other than the one on which they were made.

Dolby Myths

The fact that correct performance of the Dolby circuits depends so greatly on accurate adjustment of the deck to the tape being recorded or played back has given rise to some serious misunderstandings. The most prevalent is that Dolby dulls the highs. This is not true when everything is in proper adjustment, although even then the absence of hiss may give the illusion that some brightness has been lost.

Another misconception is that there is some benefit to recording tapes with the Dolby circuits on and playing them back with the Dolby turned off. This error may have originated from the one mentioned above, since Dolby encoding alone brightens the sound. If a tape sounds dull to you, first check to see that you have selected the correct tape type (and thus the correct playback equalization) on the deck. Then turn to your receiver's tone controls for any adjustment you think is necessary.

dbx Noise Reduction

Dolby's only real competitor is *dbx*. Unlike the Dolby systems, dbx noise reduction operates uniformly over the entire audio band, yielding a signal-to-noise improvement of approximately thirty decibels. During recording, the signal is compressed—squeezed, in effect, toward the middle—so that loud sounds become softer and soft sounds become louder. On playback, the signal is expanded back to its original dynamic range. This complete process is called *compansion*. The dbx system uses a compression ratio of 2:1, which means that signals are reduced to only half their original dynamic range before they are recorded. Effectively, it is as though the dynamic range of the tape suddenly were doubled.

The system's noise-reduction effect arises both from the higher average level at which signals are put onto the tape and from the downward expansion of soft sounds on playback, which pushes down tape hiss at the same time. In the latter respect, the operation of the dbx and Dolby systems is similar. Beyond its greater raw noise-reduction power, dbx has the advantage of requiring no sensitivity adjustment for proper operation. And on music signals, it tends to exaggerate response errors less than the Dolby systems do.

The dark side of dbx is its susceptibility to noise pumping (against which Dolby safeguards so well). For example, a loud, isolated low-frequency transient, such as a strong thwack on a bass drum, will cause upward expansion on playback. This increases the level of the tape hiss along with the drum sound, and, with no high-frequency energy in the signal to mask the hiss, it erupts briefly into audibility—as though the drum were spitting. Because of this problem, Dolby C actually sounds quieter than dbx on some material.

Partly for this reason, dbx's popularity has been fading in recent years. Another is the system's very limited portability. Tapes made with dbx encoding sound terrible unless they are decoded on playback, and the number of decks (especially car and portable models) that incorporate dbx circuitry is relatively small. Dolby-encoded tapes are listenable without decoding, and virtually all stereo cassette decks supply at least Dolby B processing.

Dolby HX Pro

Don't let the name fool you—HX Pro is not a noise-reduction system. *HX* stands for *headroom extension*. Cassettes have trouble handling loud high-frequency signals without overloading. A number of years ago, it was discovered that high-frequency energy in music has the same salutary effect on midrange distortion and headroom as a bias signal has. HX Pro takes advantage of this effect by varying the bias current according to the high-frequency content of the signal. When there is a lot of treble in the signal, the bias can be reduced slightly to improve high-frequency headroom. The biasing effect of the signal itself prevents midrange distortion from increasing. HX Pro is a valuable feature that is finding its way into increasing numbers of cassette decks. One particularly nice aspect of HX Pro is that it does not involve any playback processing. Its benefits come during recording and therefore are apparent on any deck used for playback.

Multiplex Filters

Dolby Laboratories requires that all cassette decks using their noise-reduction systems incorporate a "multiplex" (MPX) filter to remove the 19-kHz stereo pilot tone from the outputs of tuners with poor internal filtering. Otherwise, pilot leakage from the tuner might cause the noise-reduction circuits to misbehave. Although these filters do not normally have any audible effect, they do prevent response from extending to 20 kHz. Consequently, most manufacturers make the filter switchable in their top decks. Since nearly all modern tuners have adequate pilot filtering, it seldom makes any difference whether a tape deck's multiplex filter is on or off. If in doubt, leave it on.

The Tape Transport

The real centerpiece of any deck is its tape-transport mechanism. Its job is to move the tape past the heads as smoothly as possible and at the correct speed. Although it might look as though the motors attached to the hub spindles are entirely responsible for moving the tape, they really are not. The key players are a precisely ground and

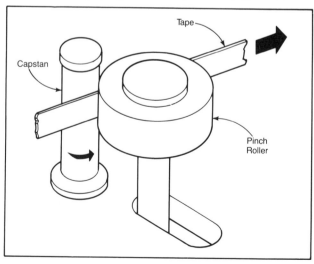

Capstan and Pinch Roller. Tape is drawn past the heads by a carefully ground and polished rod, called the *capstan*, which turns at a precisely controlled speed while the tape is pressed firmly against it by a rubber puck called the *pinch roller*.

polished steel shaft called the *capstan* and a rubber wheel called the *pinch roller.* They are placed very near the heads in such a way that the tape passes between them. During recording or playback, the pinch roller presses the tape against the capstan, which is turned by a motor to pull the tape past the heads. In fast-forward or rewind, the pinch roller retracts to allow the spindle motors to move the tape at high speed.

The roundness and smoothness of the capstan are critical to minimizing the short-term speed variations known as *flutter,* which can cause pitch instability and coarsen the sound. Some top-level decks go a step further, placing a second capstan and pinch roller at the other end of the head block. The upstream capstan turns very slightly slower than the one downstream, to keep the tape taut against the heads. The extra parts and the electronics necessary to maintain exactly the right tape tension make dual-capstan mechanisms more costly than ordinary single-capstan mechanisms.

Another feature that distinguishes different tape transports is how many motors they use and how those motors are connected to the parts they drive. It is possible, using belts, to get by with only a single motor for all functions. Most use separate motors for the spindles and the capstan, and the best employ separate direct-drive motors for each spindle and capstan in the deck. Beltless transports usually give the highest performance and reliability.

Two-Head vs. Three-Head Decks

Because the opening in the front of a cassette shell is so small, early cassette decks used only two heads: one for erasing previously recorded signals and the other for recording and playback. Later, small heads were developed that permitted the use of separate recording and playback elements, though usually mounted in the same housing for permanent accurate azimuth alignment between the two. Since the requirements for recording and playback are somewhat different, performance can be better when these functions are handled by separate heads, especially at high frequencies.

More important, three-head design enables off-tape monitoring during recording. In the tape path, the erase head comes first, the recording head second, and the playback head last, so you can listen to the signal on a tape just instants after it was recorded and without interrupting the process. This feature is very useful for checking the quality of a recording in progress (in case some adjustments are needed) and even whether the signal actually is getting onto the tape. For critical comparisons, you can use the source/tape monitor switch on the deck or your receiver to switch instantly back and forth from the input signal to the output from the tape. This capability is particu-

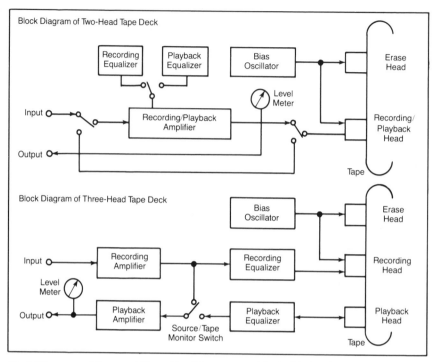

Block Diagrams of Two- and Three-Head Tape Decks. A two-head deck combines the recording and playback functions into a single head. A three-head deck uses separate recording and playback heads, enabling you to monitor the quality of a recording as it is being made.

larly handy for making bias adjustments on decks that provide no instrumentation for that purpose. If you do much recording, you'll be very pleased that you made the extra investment to get a three-head model.

Head Materials

The material used for a recording or playback head must be very hard, to minimize wear, and have good magnetic properties. Most are made of an iron compound called *permalloy* or of *ferrite,* which typically is somewhat more durable. Although the head material is important, it is more something for the design engineers to worry about than for you. Just knowing what the heads are made of will not tell you how good they are. As always, remember that the technology is just a means to an end; base your buying decisions primarily on performance, however it is achieved.

Meters and Level Setting

A vital step in making a good recording is setting input levels so that the signal going onto the tape is as strong as possible, to overcome noise on soft passages, without causing overload on loud passages. All high-fidelity tape decks provide input level controls and level meters to help you achieve this goal.

In the old days, meters looked like meters: a needle swinging in front of an illuminated, calibrated dial. These have long since been supplanted by faster, more accurate LED (light-emitting diode) indicators that show green at low and moderate levels and red at levels approaching overload. The best of these read from -40 dB (that is, forty decibels below the nominal overload level) to $+10$ dB or so and display increments of 1 dB in the vicinity of the 0-dB mark. Lower prices usually bring with them a narrower meter range and coarser divisions.

Although many user manuals advise keeping recording levels at or below the 0-dB point, there usually is some safety margin built in, enabling you to record at least somewhat "into the red" with good tape. How far you can push will depend on the tape and the music; with experience and experimentation, you can learn to judge this for yourself.

Cueing Features

The list of special features available on cassette decks to help you find your way around a tape grows longer every day. However, a couple stand out as especially worthwhile and relatively common. One is what's usually called *music search*. On your command, the deck fast-winds until it finds a blank spot on the tape—a period of two or three seconds in which there is no signal—and then drops into playback mode. This is very handy when you're trying to find a particular selection quickly.

The other feature we want to single out is a realtime tape counter—one that indicates progress through a cassette in minutes and seconds rather than in arbitrary numbers. Clearly, this is a great deal more informative and useful. Most such counters require you to indicate what length cassette you are using (C-60, C-90, and so forth), but some can figure out the tape length from the rotation rates of the hub spindles. Also, some realtime counters work during fast winds while others don't.

Autoreverse Tape Decks

Signals on a stereo cassette are laid down on four tracks, which represent a left and a right channel for each direction of tape travel. Normally, you have to take a cassette out and turn it over to record or play back in the other direction, but some decks will do the reversing for you automatically.

Two- and Four-Gap Heads. The drawing at left shows the track layout on a conventional dual-gap cassette-deck head. The one at right shows the layout for a four-gap head of the type used in some autoreverse cassette decks. The extra gaps permit recording and playback on both sides of a cassette without turning it over or rotating the head.

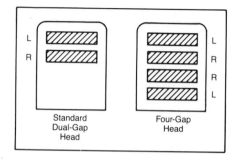

Standard Dual-Gap Head

Four-Gap Head

The easy part of this is sensing the end of the tape and reversing the tape direction. A light sensor can be used to detect the beginning of the tape leader, or a mechanical sensor can detect when the hub spindles stop turning. The former method gives a quicker turnaround, but the latter is more reliable.

The hard part is recording both sides of the tape with the same heads and without turning over the cassette. Most autoreverse decks turn the heads over instead, so that their gaps line up over the other pair of tracks. Unfortunately, it is very difficult to get the heads aligned exactly the same in both directions, with the result that performance tends to vary somewhat, especially at high frequencies. Also, the alignment will tend to deteriorate over time because of wear in the head-flipping mechanism.

Another method doubles the number of gaps in each head so that there are four instead of two—one for each track. Such heads do not need to be rotated, but they are considerably harder to fabricate and sometimes entail performance compromises of their own.

Although autoreverse decks have improved significantly over the years and can provide very good sound, their performance still does not, in general, quite match that of the best unidirectional machines. On the other hand, there can be no question of their convenience. The choice is yours.

Dual-Well Cassette Decks

A similar situation exists in the case of dual-well, or dubbing, decks. These have two complete transport mechanisms and are designed primarily to facilitate copying tapes. Some even include a double-speed dubbing option to speed up the process (though with some loss of sound quality). However, many also can be set up to switch playback automatically from one tape to another when the first one ends, for extended listening time.

As the popularity of dual-well decks has increased, so has the quality range. At first, almost all of them were cheap, relatively low-

A Dual-Well Cassette Deck

performance units designed strictly for convenience. Now you can get models that can make quite respectable recordings. However, the best performers are still conventional single-well designs.

Tape-Deck Specifications

Frequency Response
The best cassette decks are capable of response that is flat to within about ±2 dB from 20 Hz to 20 kHz with all three tape types. More typical, and still very good performance, would be 30 Hz to 15 kHz, ±3 dB. In general, response tends to be most extended with Type IV metal tapes and least extended with Type II chrome or ferricobalt tapes.

Signal-to-Noise Ratio (S/N)
Usually, Type II tapes yield the lowest noise (and therefore the highest S/N ratio) and Type I tapes yield the greatest, though the differences are seldom more than a couple of decibels. Typical figures would be around 55 dB without noise reduction, 65 dB with Dolby B, 70 dB with Dolby C, and 80 dB with dbx.

Distortion
Typically less than 1 percent at normal recording levels on a good deck. Tape overload is defined as the level at which distortion reaches 3 percent.

Speed Accuracy
Tape speed should be, at worst, within 1 percent of the correct value (1⅞ ips for cassettes). Good decks normally come within ½ percent.

Flutter
Very short-term speed variations caused by imperfections in the

motors and the capstan and by friction between the tape and the heads. The flutter specification will depend on the method used to measure it. Best is the IEEE/ANSI standard technique, but most common is the looser WRMS (JIS) method. (*WRMS* stands for *weighted RMS*.) In any event, you should expect to see figures of less than 0.15 percent (less than 0.1 percent for premium equipment).

Chapter 6

Compact Disc Players

Compact Disc Players

The Compact Disc is easily the most exciting and significant audio innovation of the last twenty years. An unparalleled combination of performance, durability, and convenience has made it the format of choice for those to whom quality of reproduction is important. Its benefits derive from the wedding of two revolutionary new technologies: optical-disc data storage and digital audio recording.

An analog recording system, such as an ordinary tape deck or a phonograph record, attempts to capture a fairly literal representation of the original sound. Putting the sound of a concert on a record is rather like taking a photograph of a house, in that sense. A digital recording, on the other hand, is more like an elaborate, finely detailed set of instructions for *building* a house. It's as though you had sent someone out with a ruler and a pad to take a lot of very exact measurements. If enough measurements are made and the ruler is accurate, you will be able to duplicate the original house, and do it better than you could if you were working from a photograph.

The same applies to digital recording. It turns out that you can actually get more accurate reproduction by measuring a signal frequently and precisely than you can by trying to capture an "image" of it, as in analog recording. This requires two basic steps—sampling and quantization—which we will explain below. Don't be disturbed if you find parts of the next couple of sections difficult to follow. The concepts underlying digital audio are somewhat abstract and usually take a while to sink in. You can even skim or skip these parts if you like. Some later discussions might be less clear to you in that case, and you will have to take more on faith, but that's all.

Sampling

What usually throws people about digital audio is the idea that you don't have to measure every point on a waveform to accurately reconstruct it later. (If that *were* necessary, the system would have to run infinitely fast, which isn't very practical!) Any waveform, no matter how complex, can be reduced mathematically to a set of simple sine waves of various frequencies and amplitudes. And since the *frequency* is just the rate at which the amplitude changes, all you really have to do is measure the amplitude often enough to assure that you don't miss any cycles of the highest-frequency sine wave in the signal.

So, how can you be sure that you've looked often enough to prevent any cycles from slipping through unnoticed? It turns out that if you measure the signal amplitude at least twice for every cycle, you're okay. In other words, the rate at which you make your measurements,

A Compact Disc Player

known as the *sampling rate,* must be at least twice the highest frequency in the signal. However, if a signal at a frequency greater than half the sampling rate does come through the system, it will cause an ugly form of distortion called *aliasing*—essentially, the result of the system getting confused and thinking the too-high frequency is a much lower one instead.

Fortunately, we know that for audio we don't need to record anything above 20 kHz (because we can't hear any sounds higher than that), so we can set the sampling rate high enough to handle that frequency and filter the input to exclude ultrasonic signals that might cause aliasing. The filters used for this purpose are known, appropriately, as *antialiasing* filters. Because these filters can't have infinite slopes, they must have some room to work, so the sampling rate has to be slightly greater than twice 20 kHz—but not too much greater, as we want to minimize the amount of information that has to be recorded. For various good reasons beyond the scope of this discussion, the sampling rate used for the Compact Disc is 44.1 kHz, or 44,100 samples per second, for each channel.

Quantization

Sampling is the first step in analog-to-digital (A/D) conversion. Before it can be recorded, each sample's amplitude must be transformed into a number, a process known as *quantization.* This is like taking a measurement with a ruler and reading it off as a number, such as "1½ inches." In digital audio, however, the numbers are binary rather than decimal, and the readings must be extremely precise.

A *binary number* is one in which each place can have only two values (0 or 1) instead of the ten possible in a decimal number. Reading from right to left, the places of a decimal number are for ones, tens, hundreds, thousands, and so on; for a binary number, these places correspond to ones, twos, fours, eights, and so on. For example, the binary number 100110 is equal to 38 in decimal notation. Binary numbers are used for data storage because they are easily represented electronically by turning circuits on and off (1s and 0s, respectively). When used for

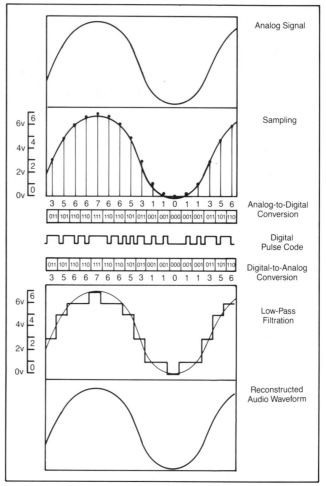

Analog to Digital and Back. Conversion of a CD's digital codes back into an analog waveform is a mirror image of the process used in the original analog-to-digital conversion. In the simplified example above, an analog sine wave is sampled sixteen times. Each sample's level is then quantized to a three-bit binary code capable of expressing eight discrete values, from 0 to 7. (The CD system uses sixteen-bit codes, for 65,536 possible values. The difference between the value of the assigned code and the actual level is the quantization error, which becomes noise on playback, so the greater the number of quantization levels, the lower the noise.) The codes are translated to a series of pulses, with up corresponding to a binary 1 and down corresponding to a binary 0. In playback, the digital code is converted to a stepped analog waveform. Low-pass filtering then removes spurious high-frequency components, leaving a signal identical to the original plus a little noise.

that purpose, each place in a binary number is called a *bit,* short for *binary digit.*

The more bits that are used, the bigger the number that can be expressed. For example, the largest possible eight-bit number is 2^8-1, or 255, whereas the largest possible twelve-bit number is $2^{12}-1$, or 4095. In digital recording, the significance of this relationship is that increasing the number of bits used to express a sample's amplitude increases the precision of that expression. It's as if you were going from a ruler marked in quarters of an inch to one marked in sixteenths. The gaps between the marks represent the uncertainty, or tolerance, of the quantization of the sample amplitudes. When the recorded signal finally is played back, that uncertainty manifests itself as noise. The finer the resolution of the quantization, the lower the noise and the wider the potential dynamic range of the recording.

The current standard for professional digital recording and the

Compact Disc is sixteen-bit pulse-code modulation (PCM). The highest-value bit is the sign bit, which indicates whether the signal is positive or negative. It is termed the *most significant bit,* or MSB. (The *least significant bit,* or LSB, is the one with the lowest value.) The total range of values available is 2^{16}, or 65,536; with the MSB serving as the sign, this becomes $\pm 32,768$. The binary numbers are represented by sequences of signals and blanks, hence the name *pulse-code modulation.*

Pros and Cons of Digital Recording

A more useful way of talking about the number of bits used in quantizing samples is in terms of signal-to-noise ratio. Each additional bit used for quantization adds about 6 dB to the S/N ratio. That gives the Compact Disc system a maximum S/N of approximately 100 dB, which is outstanding. (Signal-to-noise ratios of players usually are better still, since their circuits are designed to be quieter than the discs to assure that nothing in the signal gets masked by hiss from the electronics.) Very little music even comes close to straining its capacity.

Digital recording has other nice qualities as well. For example, if the antialiasing filters are well designed and nothing conspicuously wrong is done elsewhere, frequency response will be essentially dead flat across the entire audio band. In addition, channel separation will be extremely wide, flutter will be essentially nonexistent, and distortion will be very low. Unlike analog systems, which can gradually go out of alignment and incrementally degrade performance, digital systems tend to either work perfectly or not at all. Or if they do malfunction, they do so quite obviously.

That same quality of absoluteness accounts for one of digital's drawbacks: Digital recorders do not overload gracefully. Instead of producing gradually increasing amounts of distortion as the recording level is raised, digital recorders go abruptly from utterly clean to horrendous distortion at the point where they literally run out of numbers. So, engineers have to be more careful about these levels at digital sessions than at analog ones.

Digital recorders can also run out of bits at the bottom of the range, creating nasty distortion and an effect called *digital deafness,* which cuts off the signal abruptly at the recorder's lower limit instead of letting it tail off gradually into the noise as it would in an analog recording. Fortunately, both of these ills are easily cured with the addition of a very small amount of random noise, called *dither,* right at the recorder's lower limit. Dither has somewhat the same effect in digital recording as bias has in analog recording. It prevents both distortion and digital deafness, giving a digital recorder characteristics similar to those of a nearly perfect analog machine. Dither must be applied during recording, however; it is of no benefit if added in playback.

A Compact Disc

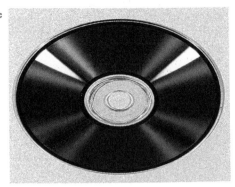

From Digits to Disc

So far, we've discussed digital audio and recording in general terms. The next step is understanding how a digitally recorded audio signal is put onto and retrieved from a Compact Disc. As the name implies, a Compact Disc is relatively small. Standard size is less than five inches across. Yet a CD, on one side, can hold more than seventy minutes of digitally encoded music. Working through the numbers, you get 44,100 sixteen-bit numbers every second for each channel. That's 705,600 bits of information per second per channel, or 1,411,200 bits per second total. So, to hold an hour's worth of music, a Compact Disc must store more than five billion bits of data, not including the extra data used for error correction and the subcode information that enables a CD player to keep track of where it is on the disc.

The formidable challenge of packing so much information into such a small space is met by using lasers to create and read the data on the disc. Optical storage enables stupendous data density. In CD mastering, a laser records the digital bit stream by selectively exposing a photoresistive coating on a glass disc. This master disc then goes through a series of processes that culminates in the generation of stampers for mass production of CDs. When the plastic backing for a Compact Disc comes off a stamper, it carries an incredibly long sequence of microscopic pits and flat areas spiraling out from near the central hole to near the rim. These pits (or bumps, depending on which side you're looking at) and flats represent the 1s and 0s of the digitally encoded audio and control signals.

The back side of the disc gets a protective coat of lacquer and a label; the other side gets a reflective coating (usually sputtered aluminum) and a layer of clear polycarbonate plastic. The polycarbonate serves both to protect the disc (it is very hard) and to help focus the laser used to read the disc. As the disc spins beneath the player's pickup laser, light reflects off the surface. From this reflected light, a photodetector senses the pits and flats that comprise the digital code.

Cutaway View of a Laser Pickup. In this design, the light from a laser diode shines through a beam-splitting prism and is focused on the aluminized information layer of a CD. Some of the light bounces back to the prism and from there into the photodetector. The weak reflection caused by a bump on the disc generates a low-voltage output from the photodetector, which translates as a binary 0. Strong reflections from flat regions of the CD are read as binary 1s.

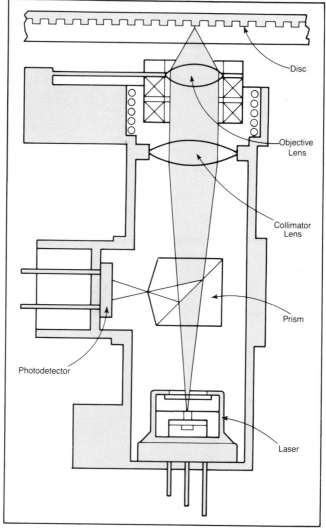

Disc

Objective Lens

Collimator Lens

Prism

Photodetector

Laser

Some of this code is for the music signal; some is for telling the player where the laser is on the disc and for controlling the disc's rotational speed and the radial movement of the pickup mechanism across the disc.

Error Correction

The data devoted to the audio signal actually contains more information than is necessary to encode the music. These extra bits are mathematically derived from the music data in such a way that they can be used to check the accuracy of the information read from the disc and actually correct nearly all the errors that are found. Although

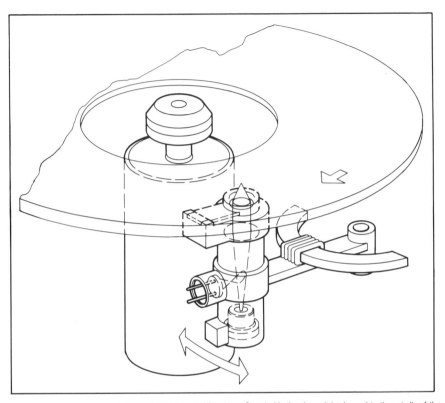

CD Player Mechanism. A Compact Disc is loaded facedown. Once inside the player, it is clamped to the spindle of the drive motor, which spins the disc at a speed that varies from 500 rpm at the center (where the recording begins) to about 200 rpm at the outer edge. This gradual reduction in angular velocity maintains a constant *linear* velocity and thus a constant data rate. The player's laser pickup swings (as shown here) or slides beneath the CD, reading it from below.

the error-correction system can fix most misreadings caused by scratches or smudges on the face of a CD, its main purpose is to repair the thousands of microscopic data defects inevitable in the molding of such fine surface details. This is important because a mistaken reading of a single bit could cause an instantaneous and inappropriate jump from almost dead quiet to full output, or vice versa, to take an extreme example. Very many such events would be distracting, to say the least.

Digital error-correction is widely misunderstood as involving some kind of approximation. In fact, it is exact. Fully error-corrected data is *identical* to the original bit stream. One also sees references to the supposed ill effects of having the error-correction system "work hard." But it actually works all the time because it is built into the mathematical processing used to sort through the data read from the disc. In other words, error-correction is something that goes on constantly as part of the process of playing back a CD and is not something you need to worry about.

Because the error-correction system is so powerful, errors drastic enough to be irreparable are quite rare on discs that are not outright defective or the victims of abuse. Many CDs contain no uncorrectable errors, and it is extremely unusual to find more than one or two on a disc. Nonetheless, that they occur at all means that the system must have some way of dealing with them, or severe distortion could result.

Here is where approximation does play a role. A backup error-concealment system comes into play, interpolating between two good samples to replace a bad one. Because of the way such "guesses" are made, they almost always are right. Even when they're not, they are unlikely to be completely inappropriate, and if too many uncorrectable errors are clustered together, the system will go mute rather than risk a big and potentially audible mistake. The upshot of all this is that CDs tend to play back correctly, not at all, or with gross and obvious malfunctions (such as skipping) rather than with subtle flaws.

Digital-to-Analog Conversion

The bit stream that emerges after error correction is strictly the music data, which now is passed to the heart of the CD player: its digital-to-analog (D/A) converter, or DAC. This converter's task is to translate each sixteen-bit number into a voltage, thereby reconstructing from the data an exact replica of the original audio waveform. The output

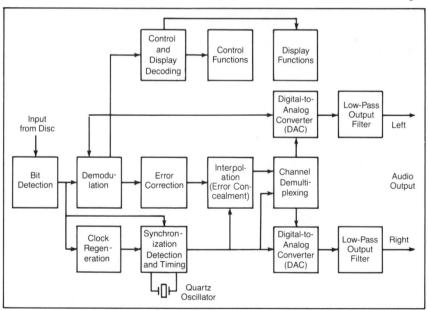

Block Diagram of a CD Player. This is what a Compact Disc player does with the data stream from a CD. There are many variations, however. For example, some players use only a single D/A converter, demultiplexing the two stereo channels at the converter's output instead of its input. And nearly all current designs place digital filters ahead of the D/A converters, relegating the analog output filters to a secondary role.

from a DAC looks somewhat unpromising in this regard, since it is stepped rather than smooth. But it is the sampling frequency and other artifacts of the conversion process that are responsible for the stepping of the waveform, and these are all ultrasonic. Filtering the output above 20 kHz removes the ultrasonic components, leaving a pristine audio signal just like the original.

Oversampling and Digital Filters

One thing you will find out immediately in shopping for a Compact Disc player is that most are touted as using four-times oversampling or eight-times oversampling or some such thing. What this means is that their D/A converters are being run at some multiple of the 44.1-kHz CD sampling frequency. Oversampling (a better name might be *resampling*) permits the use of digital filters in place of the complex and costly steep-slope analog output filters needed in a straight 44.1-kHz player. Increasing the playback sampling frequency above the standard rate opens up some room above the audio band in which a digital filter (which actually does its job before the signal enters the DAC) can operate. It is easier and ultimately cheaper to make a good digital filter than it is to build a steep analog filter right at the upper edge of the audio band that doesn't introduce significant response errors below its cutoff.

In order for an oversampling player to work, it must calculate additional "samples" from the ones actually read from the disc. For example, a four-times oversampling CD player will interpolate three extra samples for each one picked up from a disc. But no extra information is obtained, and though the output from the DAC will appear smoother, because of the closer spacing between samples, the final signal will not be any more accurate as a result. Note that even in an oversampling player, the output from the DAC is stepped: An analog filter still is needed to remove conversion artifacts. The benefit of

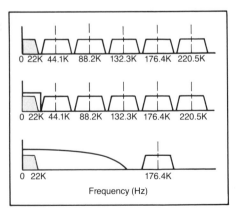

Analog vs. Digital Filtering. The process of D/A conversion generates not only the desired audio signal, but also "images" of that signal centered on multiples of the sampling frequency *(top)*. Early CD players removed this ultrasonic noise with steep analog filters *(middle)*. Usual practice now is to use oversampling digital filters ahead of the D/A converters. The digital filters suppress all images below the oversampling frequency, permitting the use of a simpler, shallower, and less costly analog filter at the output *(bottom)*.

0 22K 44.1K 88.2K 132.3K 176.4K 220.5K

0 22K 44.1K 88.2K 132.3K 176.4K 220.5K

0 22K 176.4K

Frequency (Hz)

oversampling is that this analog output filter picks up where the digital filter leaves off, near the oversampling frequency, and therefore can be shallower and simpler than the analog filter in a conventional player.

The benefits of oversampling digital filters have made them almost a standard feature in recent CD players, and out of this has arisen a numbers race that, like so many others, doesn't make much sense. Beyond a certain point, increasing the degree of oversampling doesn't buy you anything, and it may even cause trouble by forcing the D/A converters to work at speeds too close to their design limits. In short, don't think that a player that does eight- or sixteen-times oversampling is necessarily better than one that does four-times oversampling; compare their actual performance.

One DAC or Two?

Although it might seem obvious that a player needs separate left- and right-channel D/A converters, it's not true. The data on the disc alter-

Effect of Oversampling. The higher the oversampling rate used by a CD player, the less jagged the stepped outputs of its D/A converters will appear. This can give the illusion that oversampling yields higher resolution. In fact, however, the output from the final analog filtering stage (smooth curve) will be the same in every case.

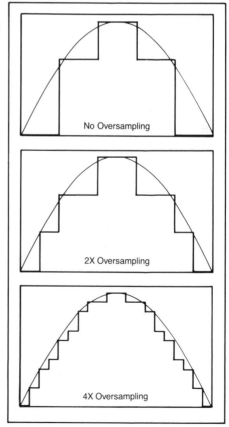

nates between channels—first one, then the other—every 11.3 microseconds, a rate of 88.2 kHz. So it is possible, not to mention economical, to use a single DAC for both, switching its output between channels in synchrony with the switching of the input. This technique works just fine, but it does cause one channel's output to lag the other's by 11.3 microseconds.

Does that matter? In stereo, no, it doesn't. It's equivalent to moving the speaker for the leading channel about an eighth of an inch forward of the other speaker, which is not something you'd ever hear. But if you mix the two channels to mono, there will be some cancellation of very high frequencies, causing a slight treble rolloff. If you're fastidious, you may prefer a player that uses separate DACs for each channel, with a delay circuit ahead of the converter for the leading channel to bring it into sync with the other. This has the added benefit of running each converter at half the rate that would be required if one were handling both channels. Consequently, virtually all players that operate with a high degree of oversampling also use dual DACs, to assure that neither is overburdened. Some players even use two DACs per channel to achieve other design goals.

Bits: 16, 18, and Beyond

Finally comes the question of sixteen-bit versus eighteen-bit and, most recently, twenty-bit D/A converters. Although you can't get more than sixteen bits' worth of information out of the data on a CD, there are reasons an eighteen-bit (or higher) converter might offer some performance advantages over a sixteen-bit DAC. It's a matter of linearity.

As we mentioned earlier, the number of bits used to quantize a sampled analog audio signal determines the resolution of the resulting *digital* signal. The more bits, the smaller the intervals between values that can be assigned to the amplitude of a sample. But the size of the intervals is not the only issue: Their evenness is also important. Again, it's like a ruler: If the scale is marked off in quarters of an inch, the space between two adjacent marks should be the same everywhere on the ruler. Similarly, a change equal to one LSB—the smallest increment the system can recognize—should give the same voltage change at the output of the DAC, no matter what the level of the signal when the change occurs. This characteristic is known as *linearity*.

Ideally, a converter should be linear at least to within ± ½ LSB over its entire range. (If this criterion is not met, it is possible that in some places a DAC's output voltage may actually go up when it should go down or down when it should go up, in which case it is said to be *nonmonotonic*.) Achieving good linearity is the biggest challenge faced in designing and manufacturing A/D and D/A converters, and the more bits the converter is supposed to handle, the harder it gets, because increasing the number of bits reduces the interval represented by an LSB.

Although there are some excellent sixteen-bit D/A converters being used today in CD players, none of them is perfectly linear over its entire range. And whatever nonlinearity is present will express itself as distortion, especially on low-level signals. One approach to minimizing the inevitable nonlinearities is to use a higher-resolution converter than is called for by the signal. For example, the LSB of an eighteen-bit DAC represents a level change only a quarter of that represented by the LSB of a sixteen-bit converter. So an eighteen-bit DAC that is linear to within ±½ LSB will be four times more linear than a sixteen-bit DAC with the same ±½-LSB specification. Or, looking at it the other way around, the smallest signal change possible from a Compact Disc is 1 LSB for a sixteen-bit DAC, whereas it is 4 LSBs for an eighteen-bit DAC.

DACs with resolutions greater than sixteen bits are being used to good advantage in many top CD players. Note, however, that a perfect sixteen-bit D/A converter would be at least as good for playing back Compact Discs as any higher-bit DAC, and it is possible for a good sixteen-bit converter to outperform a mediocre eighteen-bit chip. In other words, a player with an eighteen- or twenty-bit D/A converter is not automatically better than one with a mere sixteen-bit DAC, any more than an eight-times oversampling player is necessarily better than one that relies on four-times oversampling (or even none at all). This is something to consider when shopping for a low-price CD player, since low-quality eighteen-bit DACs are cheaper than high-performance sixteen-bit chips.

Final Touch-Ups

One particularly nasty source of linearity error is sometimes attacked directly by calibrating the D/A converter during player assembly. The problem arises whenever a signal crosses 0, since at that point the MSB changes value. Any nonlinearity in the MSB will be quite large, relative to the amplitude of the signal, when this occurs. The situation is especially bad going from −1 to 0, because the values of all sixteen bits flip over at once. DACs are temperature-sensitive enough that this abrupt change in current through the chip can throw off their accuracy. Because linearity of the MSB is so important, some manufacturers use external trimmers to adjust each converter's MSB for minimum zero-crossing distortion.

Digital Outputs

Almost all current CD players have built-in D/A converters so that they can deliver a standard audio signal to the input of an amplifier or receiver. A few, however, are designed for use with an external converter module, and, as time goes on, increasing numbers of amps and receivers will be designed to accept direct digital inputs. These components of the future will perform all the usual control and signal-processing functions (and then some) digitally, for minimum distortion and maximum flexibility. Only when the signal is ready to be amplified and sent to the loudspeakers will it be converted to analog. A small number of preamplifiers and integrated amps already have digital inputs and on-board DACs.

With the future in mind, some makers of CD players have been building in digital as well as analog outputs. Usually the digital output is a pin jack, just like those used for other audio connections, that takes a regular phono-type plug from a coaxial cable. These outputs are well standardized, with the happy result that you can almost always get one company's coaxial digital output to work with another company's coaxial digital input.

In addition to their coaxial digital outputs, some players now have outputs designed for fiber-optic cable. The digital signal is transmitted as pulses of light down a slender bundle of glass or plastic strands. Optical transmission has a number of advantages over ordinary electrical connections, including extremely wide bandwidth (important for digital audio), low loss, and immunity to RF (radio frequency) and other forms of electromagnetic interference. Fiber-optic cables are very skinny compared to ordinary audio interconnects, and you don't have to worry about things like grounding and hum. In short, they may be the wave of the future. At present, however, optical connectors are not as common as coaxial ones and are not standardized. You cannot be certain that one company's optical outputs will work with another's optical inputs.

Vibration Resistance

Although CD players are, on the whole, far less sensitive to external vibration than turntables are, they are not totally immune. A really hard jolt will cause nearly any player to skip. Some are better in this regard than others, however. Since shock-resistance is determined mainly by a player's mechanical design, you can tell a certain amount just by inspection. A sturdy, rigid chassis resting on compliant feet is going to be better than a flimsy one with no damping. But the best test is simple brute force: Don't be afraid to give a player a whack on the side and on the top, just to see how it responds.

Cuing and Taping Features

About the only thing you can't do with a CD player that you could with a turntable is reach in and move the pickup from place to place on a disc by hand. And there are so many other things that you *can* do. You can scan rapidly across a disc while listening to the output for the place you want to stop. You can skip backward and forward by track at the touch of a button. You can see at a glance how many tracks are on a disc and its playing time, the number of the track that is playing and the elapsed time within it, and in some cases the time elapsed or remaining on the disc as a whole. Many machines enable you to jump directly to a track by punching in its number on a keypad.

Anyone who likes to make tapes for his or her car or portable cassette player will recognize at once the advantages of these advanced cueing features. But a CD player can do still more for the recordist. For example, some players can be made to automatically insert a three-second pause between each track on a disc, to assure that the music-search features on most cassette decks will work properly with the tape. Less common, but more intriguing, is the ability of some players to program themselves to play just the tracks that will most nearly fill up the side of a cassette without running over. You punch in the tape length, and the player does the rest.

Programming

In fact, programmability is one of the CD system's great strengths. The player always knows where it is on a CD, because that information is embedded in the data on the disc, and the first thing a player does when it loads a CD is read a table of contents that tells it how many tracks there are, where they start, and how long they are. Almost all models can be set up to do such rudimentary things as repeat a track or a disc until you tell it to stop. And some will let you specify a number of repeats or a segment with beginning and ending points of your choosing, anywhere on the disc.

Higher up the ladder are players that enable you to program a sequence of tracks on a disc so that you can hear only the ones you want and in the order you prefer. Usually this sequence can be set for repeat-play if you like. And increasingly players are being equipped with what amounts to self-programmability: They can be set to play back tracks from a disc at random. This may sound silly at first, but it's a nice feature for parties or background music, and the variation in track order can keep you from getting bored with hearing the same sequence over and over.

CD-G and CD3

So successful has been the original Compact Disc format, and so versatile is the medium, that interesting variations have been popping up like toadstools. One of these is called CD-Graphics, or CD-G. A CD-G disc carries a series of still pictures that can be displayed on a TV screen while you listen. The content can be nearly anything, from song lyrics (in multiple languages) to interviews with performers to abstract images. The data for the graphics are carried in the disc's subcodes. Since the amount of information that can be placed there is limited, the speed with which the pictures are painted on the screen is fairly slow and the quality is like that of medium-resolution computer graphics rather than that of television.

It is yet to be seen whether CD-G will catch on. Only a handful of discs are available, and players that can make use of the graphics data are equally rare. And because the electronics needed add to the cost of a player, don't expect CD-G capability to appear in budget models anytime soon.

CD3s are three-inch discs that can hold about twenty minutes of music. Intended as a replacement for the record single, they give new meaning to the name Compact Disc. It costs essentially nothing to add CD3 capability to a player, so most recent models will load and play them without difficulty. Older units require an adapter ring that fits around the outside of the disc so that the player can handle it like a standard-size CD.

CD Changers

An increasingly popular category of players, CD changers enable you to load in a number of discs (usually between five and twelve, depending on the design) for automatic playback. Features are otherwise similar to those on single-play models.

The first changers used magazines to hold the discs. You load discs into a cartridge, which you then insert into the player. This is a particularly nice system if you have a compatible changer for your car, since you can use the same magazines at home and on the road. Also, some people find the magazines a handy storage system. Their CD collections become organized into semipermanent modules that can be changed quickly and easily. As your CD library grows, you may find storing discs permanently by category in magazines an appealing al-

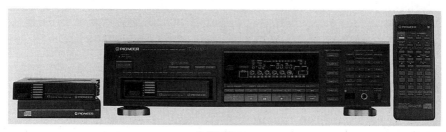

A CD Changer

A Typical Changer Magazine

ternative to keeping track of them separately. And since you don't have to handle them once you've loaded them into magazines, they are protected from accidental damage.

Recently, several manufacturers have introduced carousel changers, which have large trays that can be loaded with five or six discs. This system makes it easier to customize your selection every time you load up the player or to quickly change one or two discs. CDs still must be stored separately, however. Neither system has any innate performance advantage over the other, so which you choose is strictly a matter of personal taste.

CD-Player Specifications

Frequency Response
Although the response of some players may droop a decibel or so at the very top of the audio band (because of the output filter), most units should be within ± 0.5 dB from 20 Hz to 20 kHz. Although seldom spec'd this tightly, the very best players sometimes are within 0.1 dB over that range.

Channel Separation
By its nature, a Compact Disc has infinite channel separation. Any leakage between channels occurs strictly in the player's analog output electronics. Consequently, the separation figures for CD players typically are very high—usually 90 dB or more at midband.

This is at least three times better than is necessary. In short, it's not something you need to worry much about.

Signal-to-Noise Ratio (S/N)

CDs themselves have a maximum S/N of about 100 dB, and there is no reason for the electronics in a home player not to do at least as well. Ideally, the player's S/N should be somewhat better, to prevent any masking of low-level sounds on a disc. Figures of more than 100 dB are typical and completely adequate.

Distortion

Normally, this is specified at maximum level, and there distortion should be 0.1 percent or less. Good players usually exhibit no more than half that amount (except sometimes at very high frequencies). Distortion typically rises at lower levels, especially below −50 or −60 dB, although not usually to such a degree as to become a problem.

Linearity

Essentially another way of specifying distortion. Usually this is given as deviation from correct output level for various levels on a test disc. A good player will exhibit nearly perfect linearity down to about −60 dB, and some high-performance players hold up well down to −80 or −90 dB. However, for music reproduction, it is mostly the linearity above −70 dB that matters.

Chapter 7

CD-V and Laser Videodisc Players

CD-V *and* Laser Videodisc Players

The first application of optical disc storage was not audio, but video. Before the Compact Disc came the laser videodisc. A standard laser videodisc is twelve inches in diameter and has two playing surfaces, much like a long-playing phonograph record. Otherwise, it looks more like a CD, with shiny aluminum surfaces sheathed in protective plastic. Now there are 8-inch laser videodiscs as well, and the most recent development is a 5-inch hybrid format called CD Video, or CD-V.

Laser videodiscs stand in about the same relationship to videocassettes as CDs do to audio cassettes. You can record on tape, but the quality of reproduction from disc is much higher. (This is true, by the way, even with respect to the new high-performance videocassette formats, such as Super VHS and Hi-Band 8mm.) As on a CD, information is recorded as a sequence of pits that are read by a laser in the player. Thus, laser videodiscs share with CDs the advantage of a noncontact playback system, which eliminates wear and gradual signal degradation. A laser videodisc signal is not digitally encoded, however. Instead, a standard NTSC video signal is frequency-modulated onto the disc (rather than amplitude-modulated, as it would be for broadcast).

A Laser Videodisc Player

A Laser Videodisc

Picture Perfect?

The result is an outstanding picture. A clearly received broadcast will have somewhat less video noise, which appears as "snow" or a mottled quality in expanses of color, but laser videodiscs actually have an advantage in resolution and sound quality. This is because the laser videodisc's inherently wide bandwidth need not be compromised to fit within the limits of a broadcast channel and because the audio is recorded separately rather than on a subcarrier. The wider the video frequency response, the more detailed the picture can be along the screen's horizontal axis. This is known as *horizontal resolution.*

The NTSC broadcast system used in North America, Japan, and some other parts of the world is limited to a video bandwidth of approximately 4.2 MHz within a 6-MHz TV channel, which works out to approximately 330 lines of horizontal resolution. In other words, if the screen were the same width as height (horizontal-resolution measurements and calculations build in a correction for the screen's 4:3 width-to-height aspect ratio), a maximum of 330 discrete vertical lines could be displayed and discerned. Laser videodiscs, on the other hand, can deliver approximately 400 lines of horizontal resolution.

This kind of performance may sound like overkill at first, but as screens grow, signal quality becomes increasingly important. A good projection monitor will show you details in a picture that you probably wouldn't know were there on a typical tabletop television set. It also will show up fuzziness and other flaws that would pass unnoticed on a less-revealing display. In short, big screens need good sources.

CAV vs. CLV

There are two basic types of laser videodisc: constant angular velocity

(CAV) and constant linear velocity (CLV). (All players can handle both kinds, so you don't have to worry about that.) Television works something like movies in that motion is simulated by flashing a rapid sequence of still pictures on the screen. In TV, however, the pictures are created by scanning a modulated stream of electrons across the inside face of a tube coated with a phosphor that glows when struck by the beam. Thirty complete pictures, or frames, are scanned every second. A CAV laser videodisc spins at a constant 1,800 rpm, reading out exactly one video frame per revolution, or track. A CLV disc starts out spinning at 1,800 rpm, near the center, but gradually slows down to 600 rpm near the rim, keeping the rate at which the information on the surface passes under the pickup laser the same at all times.

The nice thing about a CAV disc is the one-to-one correspondence between frames and tracks. You can freeze the action simply by holding the laser on a track. Or you can jump to a specific frame number—a feature exploited by companies that put out discs full of still pictures related to a certain subject, such as the exploration of the solar system. But CAV is wasteful in that the outer tracks hold far less information than they could. As a result, full-size CAV discs are limited to a playing time of 30 minutes per side (three breaks in a typical movie).

CLV discs address this limitation by using the space on the disc more efficiently, thereby doubling the maximum playing time. But the neat correspondence between tracks and frames is broken, sacrificing the ability to search by frame number. And for still-frame capability, a player must have a digital memory in which to store a picture after reading it off the track. Nonetheless, their longer playing time has made CLV discs far more popular than the CAV variety for entertainment programs.

Other Cuing Features

Although search capabilities are a little more restricted with CLV than with CAV, a wide range of options remains. You can, for example, cue directly to any chapter on a disc—the equivalent of a band or track on a CD—with either format, and with CLV discs, you can cue to any elapsed-time point from the beginning of the discs, if the player supports this feature. You also can scan forward and backward at a high speed.

Recently, some of the top players have been sporting jog dials and shuttle rings. The former enable you to move, under fingertip control, forward or backward on a disc at whatever speed you like and to pause the action. This feature is much-loved by film buffs. A shuttle ring provides an easy means for varying the speed and direction of a scan. These controls are a delight, especially now that they are showing up

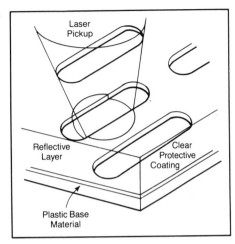

Laser Videodisc Playback

Laser Pickup

Reflective Layer

Clear Protective Coating

Plastic Base Material

on remote controls as well as front panels.

And the latest convenience feature to grace laser videodisc players is the ability of some models to switch automatically from one side to the other. Now you can watch an entire movie without stirring from your seat and with only the briefest of intermissions.

Sound

Just as the picture quality of laser videodiscs has stayed ahead of that available from tape, so has the sound. When VCRs were recording narrow-band, fluttery mono, laser videodiscs already had stereo FM soundtracks. Later, CX noise-reduction was added to many disc soundtracks to further improve performance. Hi-fi VCRs now provide stereo FM audio (AFM) tracks as well, but laser videodiscs have kept their lead by incorporating CD-style digital audio (retaining the AFM tracks for compatibility with older players). Most current laser videodisc releases incorporate both digital and AFM sound.

This digital-audio capability has spawned a new hybrid type of disc called a *CD Video.* The size of an ordinary Compact Disc, a CD-V holds a music-video clip up to five minutes in length with a digital soundtrack, followed by as much as twenty minutes of CD sound without pictures. An ordinary CD player can reproduce the audio-only portion of a CD-V, but not the music video, and a standard laser videodisc player doesn't know what to do with any of it. So to enjoy CD-Vs, you need a player designed to handle them.

Small Discs or All Discs

Theoretically, CD-V players come in two styles. One is essentially an enhanced Compact Disc player capable of reproducing the video as well as the audio but too small to accept full-size laser videodiscs. In fact, such players have not materialized. Nearly everyone interested in integrating his or her audio and video systems to the degree necessary to enjoy five-inch CD-Vs wants the ability to play full-size discs as well. So what you will find are combination CD/CD-V/LD players that take all formats in stride—everything from CD3s to twelve-inch laser videodiscs—eliminating the need for independent CD and video-disc players. And the audio performance of the best combination players is genuinely topnotch, so you don't have to feel that you've compromised by foregoing a separate CD deck. Together with a good audio-video receiver, a CD/CD-V/LD player can serve as the core of a superb audio-video system.

What's to Watch?

Because laser videodiscs are not available in as many stores as prere-corded videocassettes are, it is easy to get the impression that the se-lection is limited. In fact, thousands of titles are available, including not only movies, but also concerts, operas, educational and instruc-tional programs, and even some games. Nearly everything that comes out on videocassette also is released on videodisc.

Laser Videodisc Specifications

The comments in the last chapter about CD-player specifications ap-ply equally well to the audio performance of the latest laser videodisc players, at least with digital soundtracks. Performance will not be up to the same level on AFM soundtracks, which will play back with more noise and somewhat narrower frequency response, but since most la-ser videodiscs now have digital soundtracks, AFM is less of a consider-ation than in the past.

Horizontal Resolution
Specifications for horizontal resolution can vary greatly depend-ing on how the measurements are performed, and where VCRs and monitors (especially) are concerned, exaggeration is rampant. Anything better than 300 lines really is quite good for NTSC vid-eo, and laser videodiscs and players, at their best, are capable of nearly 400 lines.

Video Signal-to-Noise Ratio (S/N)
While resolution gets all the attention, noise is arguably a more significant factor in the quality of recorded video signals. Laser videodisc players typically are capable of video signal-to-noise ratios of 45 dB or better. This does not sound impressive com-pared with audio S/Ns, but it is good for video and better than VCRs can do.

Chapter 8

Videocassette Recorders

Videocassette Recorders

The VCR has done for television what the cassette deck did for music: made it more portable and convenient than ever before. Putting two hours of color TV on a tape cartridge the size of a large paperback book entails some compromises in picture quality, but few would argue that the results are not worth the penalty.

How VCRs Work

A broadcast television signal has a bandwidth of slightly more than 4 MHz and is amplitude-modulated onto its carrier. In addition to the main luminance signal (the black-and-white portion of the picture), which extends to 4.2 MHz, there is a vertical-synchronization pulse at 60 Hz, a horizontal-sync pulse at 15.7 kHz, a phase-modulated color subcarrier at 3.58 MHz, and an FM audio subcarrier at 4.5 MHz. Your television set takes this signal apart and uses the various pieces to put a picture on the screen and sound through the speakers. For example, the synchronization signals tell it when to go back to the top and start scanning a new screenful (field) of information and when to begin each new line within that field.

Although a home VCR that will record up to 4 or 5 MHz is practical (they all do, in fact), getting its response flat over that immense frequency range is not. This rules out direct recording like that used for audio, since the response irregularities would translate into severe distortions of the picture. Instead, VCRs frequency-modulate the video onto the tape.

But FM brings its own set of difficulties. Frequency modulation creates what are called *sidebands* above and below the FM signal itself. At least one of these sidebands must be preserved. When the first consumer VCRs were developed, the total bandwidth required to do this for a full 4.2-MHz NTSC video signal was greater than could be squeezed onto tape without making the cassette unreasonably bulky or the tape speed so high as to excessively restrict recording time. Despite improvements in both tape and recorder technology, this still is the case.

The solution has been to reformat the signal so that the unavoidable losses are as innocuous as possible. All three consumer VCR formats—Beta, VHS, and 8mm—do this in essentially the same way. The luminance portion of the signal, including the horizontal-sync pulse, is frequency-modulated onto a carrier in the vicinity of 4 MHz and is recorded along with its lower sideband. The color subcarrier is transposed down to about 700 kHz and is recorded directly, along with

A Videocassette Recorder

its sidebands, below the luminance signal (a technique known as *color-under recording*). And in the Beta and VHS formats, the vertical-sync pulse is recorded directly onto a narrow control track along one edge of the tape. (The 8mm format works this information into the video signal.) Various methods have been used to record the audio, starting with simple direct recording separate from the video on a track along the edge of the tape opposite the control track. This works, but not very well. Later in this chapter, we will discuss the much better alternatives now available.

Turning Heads

If you recall how in Chapter 5 we were impressed by audio tape decks that could achieve response to 20 kHz, you're probably wondering how one gets a 4-MHz signal onto tape that is not all that different. It takes some fancy footwork. All VCRs use rotary-head, or helical-scan, recording. A pair of tiny heads are mounted on opposite sides of a drum that spins during recording and playback. The drum is canted slightly relative to the tape, which wraps around a considerable portion of its circumference. So as the tape is pulled slowly past the drum, the heads whip across the surface of the tape. The result is a sequence of narrow diagonal tracks written at very high speed, despite the low linear speed of the tape past the drum.

The Formats

The first successful consumer VCR was the Betamax. Beta-format tapes use ½-inch tape in a fairly compact cassette. In the beginning, maximum recording time was approximately 90 minutes, which quickly put Beta on the defensive when the VHS format was intro-

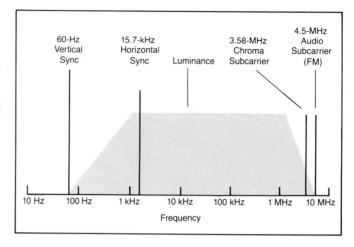

Spectrum of an NTSC Broadcast Signal. Luminance (black-and-white) information, which extends to approximately 4.2 MHz, is amplitude-modulated onto the main carrier. Color information is phase-modulated onto a subcarrier at 3.58 MHz, and audio is frequency-modulated onto another subcarrier at 4.5 MHz.

duced. VHS uses a larger cassette and a slightly slower writing speed to get two hours or more of recording time at its standard (SP) speed. It now is by far the dominant VCR format in the world.

Eventually Beta manufacturers responded with Beta II, which halved the tape speed to double the recording time. Beta II quickly replaced Beta I as the standard Beta recording speed, to the extent that now few decks will even play back Beta I tapes. Since then, a still lower extended-play mode called Beta III has been introduced, while VHS has added the LP and EP (SLP) modes, which double and triple recording time, respectively. VHS manufacturers also have brought out a camcorder system called *VHS-C,* for VHS Compact. It uses a shrunken VHS cassette with a maximum recording time of 30 minutes in SP mode. VHS-C cassettes can be played in standard VHS VCRs when inserted in a special adapter.

A few years ago, the first 8mm decks came on the market. Designed primarily for camcorders, the 8mm format uses tape eight millimeters wide—about ¼ inch. The tape also differs from that of the two ½-inch formats in employing a pure-metal, rather than an oxide, coating. This permits the use of a much smaller cassette without substantial loss of performance. Maximum recording time in 8mm's standard-play (SP) mode is two hours; a half-speed long-play mode (LP) doubles that to four hours.

Picture Quality

In general, the video performance of all three basic VCR formats might be described as adequate but not stellar, even at their highest speeds. Luminance bandwidth is limited to between 2 and 3 MHz. That's about 160–240 lines of horizontal resolution, as opposed to the approximately 330 lines available from a good broadcast. Less her-

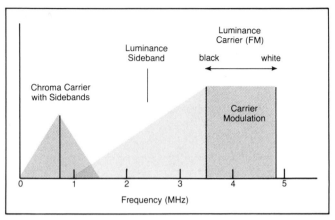

Signal Spectrum of a VCR Recording. This is how the signal was laid out on the original Beta VCRs. (With some variations, this same basic "color-under" format has been used for all consumer VCRs since.) The luminance signal is frequency-modulated onto a high-frequency carrier, while the color is moved down and amplitude-modulated onto a subcarrier just below the lower sideband of the luminance. Audio is recorded separately along the edge of the tape.

alded is the reduction in the bandwidth of the color signal. At best, the horizontal chrominance resolution of the NTSC television system is only about 120 lines, which means that fine details actually are rendered in black-and-white, even on color sets. The color resolution of the eye is not very good, so this rather poor-looking number is not unreasonable. But the color resolution of the standard VCR formats is less than half that—about 50 lines theoretically and more like 30 or 40 in practice. Video noise also is higher on videocassettes than on laser videodiscs or broadcasts, despite the use of noise-reduction systems in all VCRs. And both resolution and signal-to-noise ratio deteriorate in the low-speed, long-play recording modes.

The Super Formats

In an effort to improve performance, especially with regard to resolution, manufacturers have introduced enhanced versions of the various formats. The first of these was Super Beta, which raised the frequency of the system's luminance carrier. This, in turn, permitted a wider carrier deviation and a consequent increase in horizontal resolution. But because the system was designed to maintain nearly complete compatibility with the original Beta format (that is, Super Beta tapes were supposed to be playable on ordinary Beta decks), the carrier could not be moved far enough up to make a drastic improvement.

The VHS camp's initial, somewhat half-hearted rejoinder was VHS HQ, meaning high-quality. It consisted of several detail-enhancement and noise-reduction circuits that together made a barely noticeable difference. Much more significant was the recent introduction of Super VHS, or S-VHS. Abandoning backward compatibility, S-VHS relies on new high-density tape formulations to enable a significant upward shift in the luminance carrier frequency. Super-VHS decks boast horizontal-resolution figures in the very respectable range of 300 to 400 lines on tapes made in S-VHS mode, while retaining the

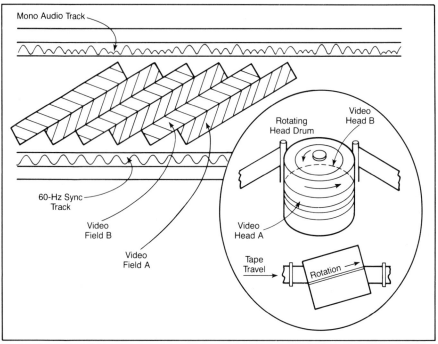

Mono Audio Track

Video
Head B

Rotating
Head Drum

60-Hz Sync
Track

Video
Field B

Video
Head A

Video
Field A

Tape
Travel

Rotation

Rotation

Rotary-Head Recording. Also called *helical-scan* recording, this technique makes it possible to record the very high frequencies needed for video on a slow-moving tape. The tape is wrapped about half way around the spinning head drum and at a slight angle. Heads on opposite sides of the drum handle the alternate fields of each video frame, laying them down on the tape as narrow diagonal tracks. The heads have different azimuths to minimize crosstalk between adjacent tracks on playback.

ability to record and play back standard VHS tapes. However, S-VHS tapes will not play correctly on regular VHS VCRs.

Following close on the heels of S-VHS came ED (extended definition) Beta, which pushes the luminance carrier higher still with benefits and limitations similar to those of S-VHS. But given Beta's dwindling significance in the market and the very high prices of all announced ED Beta machines, this new format probably is a dead end.

The new Hi-Band 8mm, or Hi8, format follows the same route to enhanced performance, with similar results. In this case, however, the patient is still breathing and promises to be invigorated by the infusion of technology.

Inputs, Outputs, and S-Video Connectors

An ordinary VCR typically has two kinds of input and output connections: RF (antenna) terminals and phono-type audio and video jacks. The former enable the VCR's built-in TV tuner to take signals from an antenna or cable hookup and to send signals to a television set without direct audio and video inputs. A direct (or composite) video connection is one that carries the video portion of a television signal after it has been stripped off the broadcast station's carrier frequency. Similarly, a direct audio connection carries the demodulated audio signal. Direct connections normally are superior to the RF variety because they minimize the number of signal-degrading trips through RF modulators and TV tuners. In addition to the usual back-panel jacks, some high-end VCRs provide an extra set of direct inputs on the front panel to facilitate copying from a source not normally in the system, such as a camcorder.

With the new "super" VCR formats has come the S-Video, or simply S, connector, which carries this idea one step further, keeping the color and luminance portions of the recorded video signal separate instead of recombining them into a standard composite output with the color on a subcarrier. This saves the monitor or whatever other device is downstream from having to reseparate the color—a good thing to avoid, because disentangling the luminance and chrominance portions of a composite-video signal is not an easy task. The frequency of the color subcarrier was chosen to minimize interference between it and the luminance signal in which it is embedded; the color information tends to fall in places where there is little luminance information. But pulling it out without damaging one or the other or getting them a little mixed up is still tricky.

One approach—now regarded, rightly or wrongly, as somewhat old-fashioned—is to put a notch filter at 3.58 MHz to remove the color subcarrier entirely from the luminance. The trouble is that you inevitably lose some response at high video frequencies in the process, degrading horizontal resolution. Replacing the traditional notch with what is known as a *comb filter,* which cancels extremely narrow, regularly spaced bands of frequencies, solves the problem by suppressing just the color information, leaving the luminance essentially untouched. It is just a matter of getting the "teeth" of the comb arranged correctly.

But comb filters tend to have shortcomings of their own. For example, they will often produce an artifact known as *hanging dots,* dots that appear to creep along a sharp horizontal color transition. Although most of us have learned to put up with this kind of mild picture distortion, it would be nice if it weren't there at all. And with an S-Video connection, it needn't be, at least for recordings in which the color and luminance have never been combined into a composite-video signal. Practically speaking, that means recordings that have been made with a camcorder. If a video signal's luminance and chrominance components have ever been melded together into a composite signal, much of the benefit of the S connection is lost.

Although S-Video connections are a good idea and worth having on your monitor and VCR, they offer only a very modest performance boost in most cases. You do not have to have S connectors on your monitor to use an S-VHS or Hi8 VCR with it, and, contrary to popular belief, they seldom afford any increase in resolution.

Still Not Ready for Prime Time

When Super VHS was announced, there was a lot of hoopla about better-than-broadcast picture quality. In fact, as good as S-VHS and Hi8 and ED Beta are, none of them is *that* good. They are significantly noisier than a good, clearly received broadcast, and they have the same restricted color resolution as their progenitors. If you're going to have a VCR, you're best off going with one of these new enhanced-performance formats, but for the best picture quality, look to laser videodisc and broadcast.

Sound

Because the linear tape speed is so low, the direct audio recording technique used in all early and current budget-model Beta and VHS VCRs produced mediocre mono sound with restricted frequency response and relatively high noise, distortion, and flutter. The movement toward integrated audio-video systems pushed manufacturers to come up with something better. First fruit of their work was Beta Hi-Fi, which squeezed four noise-reduced stereo FM audio carriers (two for each channel) between the color and luminance signals on the tape. The result was wideband, low-distortion, low-noise sound with no flutter at all.

VHS manufacturers quickly followed suit with VHS Hi-Fi, which differs from Beta Hi-Fi only in detail. It uses just two carriers, which are laid down by a separate pair of heads, as opposed to through the video heads as in Beta Hi-Fi. Performance is essentially the same, which is to say excellent.

The 8mm format started out with mono AFM (audio FM) recording as its standard system but provided for an optional stereo digital system. Except for being limited to mono, the AFM system is comparable to Beta and VHS Hi-Fi. The digital system is a companded eight-bit format, with performance approximately equivalent to that of a conventional thirteen-bit PCM system, using a 31.5-kHz sampling rate. Although not CD or laser-videodisc quality, the digital audio is quite respectable, with wider dynamic range than the AFM sound. The AFM boasts better high-frequency response, however.

The digital audio is laid down in the first one-sixth of each video head's pass across the tape, just ahead of the video track itself. This arrangement permits an interesting twist: The system can be used in an audio-only mode to record six, two-hour tracks of digital sound.

Virtually all VCRs capable of recording FM or digital soundtracks

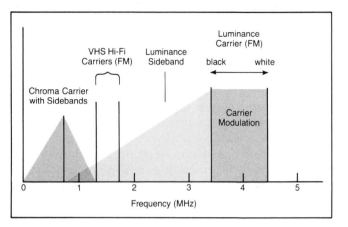

Signal Spectrum of a Hi-Fi VCR Recording. The FM carriers needed for hi-fi sound on VCRs are placed between the luminance and color signals. There is little video information in this area, so the chance of interference between the audio and video signals is minimized. This diagram is for VHS Hi-Fi; Beta Hi-Fi is very similar except that it uses two carriers for each audio channel instead of just one.

provide recoiding-level controls and meters. Unfortunately, the meter calibration is almost invariably ultraconservative, so you should push levels well up into the red, near the top of the meter's range, to minimize noise.

Head Count

The number of heads on a VCR's head drum can vary widely. A very basic machine might have just a single pair of video heads on the drum. The first four-head machines had separate pairs of heads optimized for the low and high recording speeds. Later, most manufacturers started using the extra pair of heads strictly to improve special effects, such as still-frame, optimizing them all for the slowest speed (with a consequent impairment of performance at the higher speeds). And on a VHS Hi-Fi deck, there will be an extra pair of heads for the audio, though these seldom are counted as part of the head complement. Four-head decks tend to be better than two-head models, but one can always find exceptions, so don't rely too heavily on the head count as an index of performance.

The Tuner/Timer

Virtually without exception, VCRs include TV tuners similar to those in a television set. The tuner picks up signals from your antenna or cable system, singles out the one of your choice, and demodulates it into audio and composite-video signals. And tuners in VCRs capable of recording high-fidelity stereo sound normally are designed to properly receive the stereo audio now being transmitted by some stations. (TV tuners and MTS stereo sound for television are discussed in more detail in the next chapter.) Even very early VCRs included a timer feature that enabled you to set the machine for unattended recording.

Initially, this was about the only reason to own one, unless you wanted to collect recordings of programs from off the air.

As the model years passed and maximum recording times were extended, the timer function became increasingly elaborate on all but the cheapest VCRs. Today, most VCRs can be programmed to record a sequence of programs at different times on different days and channels—often as many as eight over a two-week period. If you are mainly interested in playback of prerecorded tapes, a programmable timer doesn't matter much, but if you plan to do a significant amount of unattended recording off the air, you should pay careful attention to how the VCRs you're considering implement this feature.

Most important to remember is that quantity (number of events and days that can be programmed) is not the only issue. In particular, how easy is it to program the VCR? The feature is useless if you can't make it work. Onscreen programming, in which a series of menus on the television screen leads you through the process, has become increasingly popular. But even these systems vary widely in quality. It's a good idea to try before you buy: Have the salesperson step you through the procedure so that you know exactly what you're getting into.

Special Effects

Most of today's videocassette recorders are capable of at least a few basic special effects, such as stop-action (still-frame), slow-motion, and fast scan forward or backward at one or more speeds with a picture. Although picture quality always deteriorates somewhat in these modes, the best machines do a good job of minimizing the loss. How many people actually use features like slow-motion with any regularity is an open question, but a basic fast-scan feature is extremely handy when you're looking for a specific scene or program on a long tape.

Of more dubious value are the "artistic" digital effects that recently have come into vogue. Some VCRs enable you to give the picture a broken-up mosaic-like appearance or to drastically modify the coloration of the image—interesting to see once or twice. On the other hand, the digital technology behind these throwaway features can render genuine benefits as well. For example, some VCRs now use digital image storage to provide noise-free still-frames or to inset a small picture from one source (such as the TV tuner) into a corner of the screen while the rest is occupied by a picture from another source (such as a tape). The latter feature is called *picture-in-picture,* or PIP. A few VCRs even use digital techniques to reduce picture noise, though this can cause image smearing if overdone.

Editing Aids

We won't attempt an exhaustive list of advanced features available on

VCRs: It would be too long. However, if you like to shoot home videos with a camcorder, you may like the editing facilities on some top decks. These include edit switches that reduce the amount of equalization applied to the video signal (to enhance detail), which can help minimize the image degradation associated with copying from tape to tape. And a growing handful have jog dials that enable you to scan through a tape very slowly or at very high speed and flying erase heads (on the drum with the record/play heads) for clean transitions—very nice when you're trying to make a tight edit.

Look Before You Leap

Getting the features you want is important, but once you've settled on a must-have list, it's time to think about performance again. Most VCRs with hi-fi (AFM) or digital audio capability provide a very similar and quite acceptable level of sound quality. Variations in picture quality are more pronounced, however, even within a format. That is, you may find two otherwise similar S-VHS (or Beta or 8mm) decks that nonetheless differ noticeably in their ability to make a clean, crisp recording of a video image.

Test results and specifications can help, when they are available, but it doesn't hurt to trust your own eyes. The best approach is to compare the VCRs you're interested in by recording on each of them from the same source (such as a laser videodisc) and then facing the tapes off against the original and each other on a good monitor through its composite or S-video inputs. (Make sure when you do this that sharpness controls and so forth on both the decks and the monitor are at their normal settings.) Look for such flaws as loss of fine detail, graininess, color shifts, mottling or instability in large fields of color, and overenhanced edges that make objects look outlined on the screen. Try to find the best combination of sharpness, smoothness, and overall naturalness of reproduction.

Grades of Tape

Like audio tape, video tape comes in various grades. The most important line of demarcation is between tapes designed for the regular formats (Beta, VHS, and 8mm) and the souped-up formulations required by the superformats (ED Beta, S-VHS, and Hi8). For example, an S-VHS tape is okay (though costly) for standard recording, but a regular VHS tape cannot handle the high frequencies necessary for S-VHS recording.

Within these two broad categories, the distinctions often are less clear. Tape manufacturers usually sell a line of several different formulations in each. Although the top grade will outperform the bottom one, the visible and audible distinctions may be subtle, especially between two adjacent grades in a line of five or more. As long as you choose a reputable brand, you can be fairly certain that you will not encounter any serious shortcomings in even the budget formulation. A common, reasonable strategy is to use an inexpensive grade for day-to-day time-shift taping and a top grade for recordings you value enough to save. Avoid off-brand tapes, as these often are of inferior quality. They may deliver poor picture quality, wear out prematurely, or shed oxide, possibly clogging the heads of your VCR.

VCR Specifications

Horizontal Resolution

Resolution figures can vary according to how the measurement is made, but most of the ones you will see are toward the high side of what the machine actually can achieve. For regular Beta, VHS, and 8mm, a typical rating would be 240 lines, a conservative one perhaps about 160 lines. None of these formats can match broadcast resolution, so there is some loss of sharpness. For ED Beta, S-VHS, and Hi8, the numbers could range from approximately 330 lines to nearly 400, which means that these formats are close to broadcast in resolution.

Video Signal-to-Noise Ratio (S/N)

VCRs typically have S/Ns in the range of 42 dB. This looks dreadful compared to audio noise figures, but it isn't bad for video. Although seldom given the same prominence as resolution, noise performance is at least as important to picture quality.

Audio Frequency Response

The response of hi-fi, or AFM, recording typically is quite good—very smooth and flat with slight rolloffs at the extremes of the audio band. It is seldom down more than a couple of decibels at 20 Hz and 20 kHz. Response of the digital audio tracks available on some 8mm decks is nearly as good but rolls off sharply above about 14 kHz. Worst by far is the response of direct edge-track recording. At best, it extends from approximately 50 Hz (where it already will be down about 5 dB) to perhaps 12 kHz at the highest speed. Response at the lowest recording speed will not get past 7 kHz or so and will not be very flat.

Audio Signal-to-Noise Ratio (S/N)

Expect figures of approximately 70–80 dB for hi-fi, or AFM, recording and possibly a few decibels better for 8mm digital. The direct linear-track recording used on non-hi-fi Beta and VHS decks will come in at less than 50 dB.

Distortion

Hi-fi, or AFM, recording is the champ here. Distortion usually is less than 1 percent at midband and often less than ½ percent. The 8mm digital system is nearly as good, with figures of a little more than 1 percent being typical. Again, edge-track recording is by far the worst; its distortion is seldom better than 3 or 4 percent.

Flutter

Hi-fi, or AFM, and digital recording are completely free of flutter. Edge-track recording, on the other hand, is pretty bad in this respect, with figures ranging from 0.1 to 0.5 percent. Audibly obvious flutter is not uncommon in this mode.

Channel Separation

With hi-fi or digital recording, separation usually is better than 70 dB, which is much more than adequate for full stereo effect.

Chapter 9

Video Monitors

Video Monitors

Like a table radio, a run-of-the-mill TV set plucks signals from the air and then extracts from them the information they carry and presents it to you in a form you can use. Some perform these functions a little better than others, but for the most part, the picture and sound you get are undistinguished. You don't see and hear all that is in the broadcast signal, and what you do see and hear probably is not as clear and accurate as it might be. It took the development of high-performance large-screen projection television sets and high-quality nonbroadcast sources, such as laser videodiscs, to suggest the potential of the medium most of us have taken for granted all our lives.

The result has been a small but growing number of video monitors (displays without internal TV tuners) and monitor/receivers (which include tuners as well as external inputs) designed to provide high-fidelity reproduction of video images. In the beginning, these products could be identified simply from their jack panels, which typically provided direct audio and video inputs missing from conventional sets. These inputs permitted slightly higher quality from VCRs and laser videodisc players than could be realized by routing their signals through the standard RF (antenna) terminals. As this feature has spread, however, the only real distinguishing trait has become the vividness of the image on the screen.

Unfortunately, attention has tended to focus on one narrow measure of performance to the virtual exclusion of all others. There is a widespread assumption that resolution is the whole shooting match. It *is* important, but just as distortion or frequency response does not, alone, tell the whole story on a loudspeaker, neither does a resolution specification tell you all you need to know about a monitor. To understand the various elements that must come together properly to form a good television image, you need to know a little about the way monitors operate.

How Monitors Work

In the NTSC television system (used in North America, Japan, and some other parts of the world), the video part of the signal conveys a series of thirty complete still images every second, simulating motion in essentially the same way as a movie. A key difference, however, is that film images are formed all at once, whereas each complete video image, or frame, is generated by a process known as *scanning*. It is built up line by line over the period of time it will occupy the screen. This occurs first in the video camera shooting the scene and again, later, in the monitor on which it is viewed.

A Direct-View Monitor

In a monitor, the image is scanned by an electron beam that sweeps across the inside surface of a cathode-ray tube (CRT), which is coated with phosphors that glow when struck by the beam. The greater the intensity of the electron beam at any given moment, the brighter the phosphor will glow at that point. In a black-and-white (monochrome) set, the coating is uniform and the picture is built up of simple variations in brightness (luminance).

Formation of a color picture is more complex but similar in concept. It depends on the ability to generate any color by combining three primary colors in various proportions. In a conventional direct-view monitor (one with a picture tube that you look right at), the inside of the screen is painted with thousands of tightly spaced triads of red, green, and blue phosphor dots. Instead of a single electron beam, there are three, each dedicated to one of those colors. Varying the relative intensities of these three beams produces different amounts of light from their phosphors. Although you can see the individual dots from very close up, at any reasonable viewing distance, the light from the three dots in a group merge into a composite color determined by the exact mix of the three primary colors. Projection monitors (which

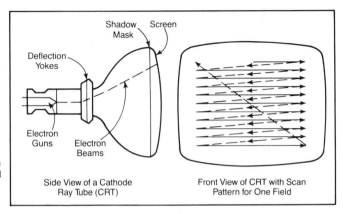

Scanning a TV Picture. A television picture is created by scanning an electron beam across the phosphor-coated inside face of a CRT (cathode-ray tube) in a pattern like that shown at right. Two complete passes *(fields)* are required to generate one complete still image *(frame)*, with the lines from the second pass falling between those of the first. The movement of the electron beam is controlled by electromagnets in the yoke around the neck of the CRT *(left)*.

Shadow Mask — Screen

Deflection Yokes

Electron Guns — Electron Beams

Side View of a Cathode Ray Tube (CRT)

Front View of CRT with Scan Pattern for One Field

we will discuss in more detail a little later) achieve the same effect by somewhat different means, mixing the outputs from separate red, green, and blue tubes.

Interlace

In the NTSC television system, 525 lines are scanned horizontally across the screen in each frame. This number together with the frame rate (the number of frames displayed per second) and the bandwidth of the video signal determine the amount of information that can be displayed. The bandwidth is important because no change can occur on the screen unless the video signal has changed. And since the electron beam is sweeping continuously across the inside of the tube, the number of changes in brightness and color that can occur on a scan line is determined by the maximum number of cycles the video signal can go through during the period in which that line is being put up. The wider the bandwidth of the video signal, the more cycles it can complete per scan line and the more detail the monitor can display.

There must be some limit on the video bandwidth, if only because increasing the bandwidth of the signal reduces the number of channels that can be placed in the portion of the RF (radio frequency) spectrum allocated to television. The frame rate and number of scan lines used in the NTSC television system were chosen to provide adequate picture detail with a signal that can fit comfortably in a 6-MHz channel. Unfortunately, scanning only thirty frames per second yields a picture that flickers terribly. The solution is a system called *interlaced scanning,* in which half a frame (a 262.5-line field) is scanned every sixtieth of a second. When the monitor has finished scanning the first field of a frame, it sends the electron beams back to the top of the screen and scans the second field, whose lines fall exactly in between the lines of the first. Interlaced scanning is not a perfect solution (you can still see some flickering of individual lines, for example), but on the whole, it is an elegant and effective technique.

Vertical Resolution

The amount of detail that a video component can convey is called its *resolution,* which is given as the maximum number of vertical or horizontal lines that can be displayed across a distance equal to the height of the screen. Vertical resolution (the amount of detail from the top of the image to the bottom) is determined primarily by the number of scan lines. Of the 525 scan lines in an NTSC frame, about 480 are used for picture information; the rest fall into what is known as the *vertical blanking interval,* which is used for synchronization of the picture.

It might seem, therefore, that the NTSC system allows for a maximum vertical resolution of approximately 480 lines. In practice, however, it's lower than that. The eye doesn't resolve the vertical detail in a scanned image as well as it does in one that is not scanned (such as a photograph). The degree of loss varies according to the amount of motion in the scene and other factors, making precise specification of the system's maximum vertical resolution impossible. It is usually taken to be somewhere between 330 and 400 lines. Regardless of the exact number, just about any properly functioning video component should deliver full vertical resolution. For monitors, the key is correct interlace. If any of the lines in two successive fields overlap, instead of falling exactly between each other, there will be some reduction of vertical resolution. Fortunately, this is rare.

Horizontal Resolution

When you see a resolution specification, it usually will be for horizontal resolution, which is more variable. In a monitor, horizontal resolution depends on two things: the bandwidth of the video circuitry and what is known as the *dot pitch* of the screen. The latter is simply the spacing between the clusters of phosphor dots. For a given size of screen, the tighter the spacing between dot clusters, the greater the horizontal resolution the screen can display.

In high-performance monitors, the dot pitch usually is the limiting factor as far as horizontal resolution is concerned, but the electronics can make a difference as well. For one thing, the luminance response of the video circuitry should be at least great enough to handle the entire 4.2-MHz bandwidth of an NTSC television broadcast, and response to 5 MHz or so is worthwhile if you want to wring the last iota of detail from a top-notch laser videodisc. The rule of thumb is that, screen permitting, you get 80 lines of horizontal resolution for every megahertz of video bandwidth.

There is another consideration, however. When color was added to our originally black-and-white television system, the additional information needed was packed onto a subcarrier at 3.58 MHz—smack in the middle of the luminance signal on the main carrier. Separating the signal on the subcarrier from that on the main carrier without damaging either is a vital but tricky part of the reproduction process.

One approach is to use a notch filter centered on 3.58 MHz. This technique is clean and relatively simple, but it does put a hole in the top of the luminance response, sacrificing some fine picture detail. A more sophisticated method is to use what is known as a *comb filter,* which is much more selective in its action. Monitors that employ comb filters do not suffer from the slight loss of detail that attends notch filtering, but they are more complex and therefore more costly. They also are prone to artifacts arising from interference between chrominance (color) and luminance signals at sharp transitions between colors. For example, onscreen graphics tend to produce dots that crawl up or across their edges. The severity of these side effects depends on the quality of the filter and the nature of the signal. Some monitors provide a switchable notch filter that can be inserted to control such artifacts when they become severe enough to be objectionable.

It is not uncommon for people to treat horizontal luminance resolution as if it were the sole important performance characteristic of a monitor. This misconception has fueled an often pointless resolution race. A high-performance monitor should be capable of reproducing at least the 330-line resolution of broadcast TV. One that can manage 400 lines is outstanding and up to the demands of virtually any program material you can throw at it.

Color Resolution

A little-known fact about television is that the color resolution is much lower than the luminance resolution—that is, lower than the resolution of the black-and-white part of the picture. The bandwidth of the signal on the chrominance subcarrier is at most about 1.5 MHz, which translates to approximately 120 lines of horizontal color resolution if the monitor uses a full-band demodulator (most don't). Technically, this means that the total output from the three electron beams (which determines brightness at any given point) can change several times more often than their relative outputs (which determine color). The color resolution of our eyes is much worse than their monochrome resolution, so this arrangement is quite sensible and doesn't impair the system's ability to render detail.

Overscan

To assure that the picture always fills the entire screen—even when the load on the power supply increases (because of a switch from a dark to a light scene, for example) or the voltage on the power line dips—all monitors and television sets are designed to overscan somewhat. The edges of the image are actually placed beyond the visible edges of the screen, reducing the amount that you see. A conventional television set may overscan by 20 percent or more. For this reason, all television programs are shot so that important action falls near the middle of the screen, in what is known as the *safe area*. With good power-supply design, it's possible to reduce the amount of overscan without risk of ever showing a border around the picture. A good monitor should overscan no more than about 10 percent, and the best hold it to around 5 percent.

Geometric Accuracy

Besides showing as much of the picture as possible, a good monitor should display it with minimum distortion. Straight lines should be straight, circles should be perfectly round, and so forth. Achieving this is much harder than it sounds. (You probably have seen sets on which the tops of people's heads looked too big, for example.) Look carefully before you buy.

Convergence

Correct reproduction of a color television picture requires precise alignment of the three primary-hue images from which it is formed. Otherwise, they won't fuse properly and you will see color fringes around objects on the screen. In a direct-view monitor, the three electron beams must be focused very accurately; in a projection monitor, it is the aiming of the individual tubes (for red, green, and blue) that matters. In either case, convergence normally tends to be best near the center of the screen and worst near the corners. And all else being equal, maintaining good convergence typically is more difficult for large screens than for small ones. This is not to say, however, that convergence will necessarily be worse on a big screen than on a little one; the shoe can even be on the other foot. Design and construction quality, as well as the care with which the monitor is adjusted at the factory, are critically important. Better sets will exhibit better convergence.

Gray-Scale and Black-Level Accuracy

The foundation of a good television picture, color or not, is first-rate black-and-white performance. One aspect of this is gray-scale linearity: the ability to portray the range from deep black through ever-lightening shades of gray to pure white smoothly and completely. Another, related characteristic is a monitor's ability to keep black areas black, especially when some areas of the screen are bright. On many sets, the screen tends to gray-out large areas of darkness, reducing the detail and impact of a scene showing stars against a night sky, for example. This problem usually is easy to spot if you're looking for it.

Color Accuracy

These days, we usually expect a monitor to display colors accurately, as well. Unfortunately, none of the monitors available to consumers today can display the full range of colors the NTSC television system is capable of handling, although projection monitors usually are better in this regard than direct-view sets. Some sacrifice has been accepted in the quest for a picture bright enough to be viewed in a daylit room. Most apparent is the tendency for reds to be slightly orange.

These limitations aside, however, a modern high-performance monitor should be capable of delivering very true colors when adjusted properly. The most common problem is an excessively blue picture, which results from too high a *color temperature*. Despite its name, color temperature determines the exact mix of hues that comprise white, not how hot the CRT runs or something like that. Raising the color temperature makes the mix bluer, whereas reducing it moves the balance more toward red. Standard color temperature for NTSC displays is supposed to be 6,500 degrees Kelvin. That arguably is a little too red, but one sees monitors with color temperatures set to 9,000 degrees or more, which definitely is too blue.

Inputs and Switching

Unless you buy a monitor that does not have an internal TV tuner (very rare outside the professional market), you'll have at least a set of VHF and UHF antenna inputs. You can use the VHF input to hook up your VCR and laser videodisc player also, but that's neither the best nor the most convenient way. Look for a monitor/receiver with at least two sets of direct audio and video inputs. Signals passed through these inputs are spared the degradation of an unnecessary cycle of RF modulation and demodulation, and you can switch easily between them and the built-in TV tuner.

You can realize another, smaller increment of improvement by attaching your VCR to your monitor with S-video connectors, which made their first appearance when Super VHS was introduced. Most monitor/receivers now have S-video inputs along with the usual composite and RF connectors. They can also be used with suitably equipped laser videodisc players, but the benefit, if any, will be smaller. Try both methods and stick with the one that looks better.

Other common and desirable features of monitor receivers are an extra, switchable VHF input, at least one set of stereo audio outputs, and a set of front-panel audio-video inputs for attaching a camcorder or other source for playback. The additional antenna connector is handy if you need a descrambler for certain pay channels but want to tune the others in the usual way (and spare them an unnecessary trip through the video circuitry in the decoder). The audio outputs are enormously helpful if you're setting up, or planning to set up, an integrated audio-video system, since it centralizes the switching for video sources. And the front-panel inputs are very handy if you have, for example, an 8mm camcorder but no 8mm VCR.

The TV Tuner

One of your video sources is almost certain to be broadcast or cable television. A TV tuner is basically very similar to a radio tuner. Its job is to take the signals that come in from an antenna or cable feed, discard all those except the one you have tuned, and then remove that desired signal from its RF carrier and send it to the monitor electronics in a form they can process. This last stage separates the composite-video signal, which carries luminance and color information, from the audio, which is on a frequency-modulated subcarrier at 4.5 MHz, just slightly above the 4.2-MHz upper limit of the video signal. The tuner simply passes the composite-video signal to the monitor, but it finishes the job on the FM audio signal, demodulating it into a standard audio output that can drive an internal power amplifier for the monitor's built-in speakers or feed an external audio system.

Today's high-performance monitor/receivers typically have digital frequency-synthesis tuners that select channels precisely with a minimum of fuss and bother on your part. And virtually all of them are cable-ready, with the ability to tune virtually any channel you'll ever encounter.

Stereo TV Sound

Poor broadcasting practices and cheap, limited-range speakers in TV sets have tended to mask the fact that television sound has always had the potential to be pretty decent. Practically speaking, its upper frequency limit is about 12 kHz, imposed by the need to filter leakage of the 15.7-kHz horizontal-sync frequency out of the signal. Signal-to-noise ratio (S/N) is not high by the standards of FM radio, but it is adequate for the highly compressed sound generally preferred for television. And until recently, it was always mono.

The MTS (Multichannel Television Sound) standard changes that by enabling the transmission of low-noise stereo audio that is compatible with the old mono system. It also provides for a lower-fidelity mono SAP (Secondary Audio Program) signal that can be used for bilingual broadcasts or to carry an entirely separate audio program. Most high-quality television sets and monitor/receivers, as well as hi-fi VCRs, now have MTS-compatible tuners, and the number of television stations and programs taking advantage of the system has been steadily increasing. There have even been a few experiments with broadcasting Dolby Surround, which can be folded into any stereo signal.

Large-Screen Television

A key step in buying a monitor is deciding how big it should be. The trend in recent years has been to larger and larger screens, to the point where you can now buy sets with thirty-five-inch direct-view picture tubes. Still larger images—up to ten feet diagonally, in some cases—are possible with projection monitors. That might sound like overkill, but there's no question that big screens pack a more dramatic wallop than little ones.

The most important single difference between projection and direct-view monitors is that projectors typically use separate tubes for red, green, and blue. This is necessary to obtain adequate brightness on a large screen with tubes of reasonable size. Design of the tubes also is critical. The number of lenses and other optical elements in the path between the CRTs and the screen must be minimized to maintain efficient light transmission. Efficient cooling of the tubes also is important, since this permits the use of higher-voltage electron beams to increase light output. In addition, correct alignment and focus of these tubes is crucial to maintaining sharpness and convergence.

The other big difference between direct-view and projection monitors is the screen. In a direct-view set, the face of the CRT is the screen. A projection unit, on the other hand, focuses the output of its three CRTs through lenses to strike a larger screen some distance away. In a two-piece front-projection system, the projector is completely separate from the screen and set up in front of it. The image reflects off the screen, much as in a movie theater.

Two-piece systems are somewhat cumbersome and require careful installation for good performance. As a result, one-piece rear-projector systems, which set up like a large conventional television set,

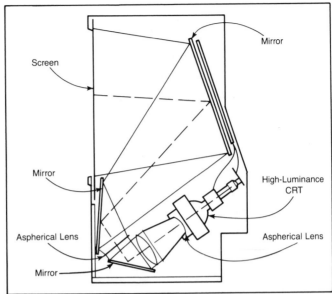

Inside a Rear-Projection Monitor. Images are formed on the inside of the screen by bouncing the outputs from three CRTs (one each for red, green, and blue) off a series of mirrors.

are much more popular, especially now that manufacturers are figuring out how to reduce their bulk. In a rear-projection system, the light from the tubes is reflected by mirrors onto the inside surface of a translucent screen. Early monitors of this type looked rather grainy and lost brightness and color accuracy rapidly as you moved from directly in front of the screen to the side. Improvements in the design of the screens have reduced these problems to the point where they are no longer much of an issue when considering the best examples of the genre. And because the screen is perfectly flat, glare is less of a problem than with direct-view monitors. For best results, however, you should sit somewhat farther from a projection monitor than you would from a standard-size direct-view set.

Shopping and Setup

Buying a monitor is a lot like buying loudspeakers: Although specifications and features may help you narrow your list of candidates, they cannot substitute for a hands-on evaluation. You must look before you buy. But look carefully. Make sure demonstrations are conducted with topnotch source material (a clean, well-received broadcast or a good laser videodisc), and don't take it for granted that the store has all of the monitors adjusted optimally. In fact, you shouldn't even trust the manufacturer's default or automatic control settings. For example, many monitors are delivered with their color controls set too high. This makes them stand out on the shop floor, but it isn't natural and is hard on the eyes. And automatic flesh-tone correction circuits work by pulling all colors in a certain range to the same value, regardless of

A Rear-Projection Monitor

whether the place occupied by the color is really someone's skin.

The best approach is to do what you should at home. Start by turning the color all the way off and adjusting the brightness and contrast controls for the best black-and-white picture you can get. Whites should be white, and blacks should be black, with plenty of detail even in dark areas. Next turn up the color control until colors seem about the right intensity. Then adjust the tint control for as natural a color balance as you can get. Another round or two of the controls for fine-tuning your settings, and you should have a very nice color picture. Once you've done this with all the sets you're interested in, take your time deciding which one makes the most pleasing and lifelike picture. Just as you have to trust your ears when you buy loudspeakers, you have to trust your eyes when you buy a monitor.

Monitor Specifications

Horizontal Resolution

A measure of the amount of detail that can be displayed across the screen, given in lines. A good broadcast can deliver about 330 lines of resolution on a monitor that is up to the task. Conventional low-price television sets typically poop out at about 240 lines. A high-performance monitor should do at least 330 lines, and most are rated at 400 lines or more. Monitor resolution greater than that is fine, but given the limits of available source material, it is gilding the lily. A difference in resolution specifications should never be the sole reason for choosing one monitor over another.

Brightness

Usually specified only for projection monitors. Early projectors often had brightness specs in the range of 120 to 150 foot-lamberts, which meant they could be viewed well only in dimly lit rooms. Brightness figures of 200 or even 300 foot-lamberts are more typical now. Unfortunately, there is no standard for measuring screen brightness, so you can't really go by the numbers. You're best off judging it by eye. (Bear in mind, however, that even direct-view sets will look their best if adjusted and viewed in a room that is not brightly lit.)

Viewing Angle

Another specification relevant mainly to projection sets. This is the angle over which the set can be viewed without serious loss of picture quality. A fairly narrow vertical angle is not so bad, since you're likely to be sitting down when watching, but the horizontal angle can make a big difference in how practical a particular monitor is for you. You should consider 80 degrees a minimum, but 100–120 degrees is much better.

Chapter 10

Signal Processors
and Accessories

Signal Processors and Accessories

Although you can put together a very complete audio-video system from the components we've already discussed, you don't have to stop there. One of the great advantages of a component system is its expandability. You can modify and add onto it, often in ways not originally envisioned by you or by any of the manufacturers of your equipment. With that in mind, let's turn to some of the currently available extras you might want to consider.

Remote Control

In its most common form, a remote control is not an accessory except in the sense that it isn't physically part of the component that it operates. Occasionally a remote is an extra-cost option, but most products that can be worked from a distance come with one packed in every box—usually one that functions with that product only. Such dedicated remotes have spread lately from their initial beachhead among television sets and VCRs to virtually all CD players selling for more than a few hundred dollars and to many high-end receivers and other audio and audio-video components. Almost without exception, these remotes are wireless devices that function by sending pulses of infrared light to a receiving sensor on the product being controlled.

The one problem arising from this proliferation of remote control is clutter—an unsightly buildup of dedicated remotes. Fortunately, there are a couple of solutions. Some manufacturers make it possible for you to control multiple components from a single multipurpose handset, either by building sensors into many of their products or by providing wired control links between a central component (such as a receiver) and others in the system. Normally, however, this approach works only for products from a single manufacturer; mixed-brand systems need not apply.

A more general and increasingly popular cure for remote clutter is a universal, or learning, remote control. These wonderful, button-laden devices can memorize and then mimic the control codes from most dedicated wireless remotes, virtually regardless of brand, enabling you to consolidate their functions into a single handset. Some manufacturers have taken to making the remote control included with some of their products a programmable model, but they also are available separately.

This is good because it gives you a choice in a field where not all are created equal. Providing for nearly all the functions you might find on any collection of audio and video components without making the

control unreasonably complicated and confusing is a formidable challenge. So try before you buy. Make sure you can reach all the buttons easily, that the buttons aren't too small or crowded, and that their arrangement is logical. The remote remembers all the necessary control codes, but you have to remember which button to push for each function, especially for unusual ones that you may have to assign to buttons not specifically marked for them. Some universal remotes come with templates that you can label and fit over the keys to help you remember what each one does.

Although remote control is still considered a luxury feature, it is almost a necessity for achieving proper setup of a surround-sound system. In fact, any adjustment whose effect may vary according to where you are sitting or standing is best made from the listening position. That category includes tone-control and equalizer adjustments—even something as simple as setting channel balance.

It's also a wonderful thing to have when you're in a room with a pair of extension speakers and the components feeding them are in another room. This has lead to the development of multiroom remote-control systems. Usually these employ sensors that transmit the infrared signals from a remote-control handset down wires to a repeater in the room holding the main system. Such a system can be surprisingly inconspicuous and affordable.

Equalizers

Probably the most popular type of add-on component is an equalizer. Basically, an equalizer is a super tone control, offering you greater flexibility and precision in altering frequency balance. By far the most common type is the graphic equalizer, which enables you to raise or lower the amount of energy in each of a number of bands centered on fixed frequencies. Usually there are controls for ten bands with center frequencies spaced at octave intervals, but some low-price models may have as few as five bands. Graphic equalizers with a large number of bands offer the greatest control over tonal balance, but, naturally, they also require the greatest effort to adjust.

The other main type is what's known as a *parametric equalizer,* because of its extreme flexibility. Usually a parametric equalizer has controls for only two or three bands, but everything about its action is adjustable: the widths and center frequencies of the control bands as well as the amount of boost or cut in each one. This makes a parametric equalizer ideal for very precise alterations in frequency response but, again, more difficult to use.

Equalizers have two basic functions in an audio system. The more ambitious is to smooth out response irregularities introduced by the acoustics of the listening room, especially at low frequencies. Some models even come with a microphone and a built-in spectrum analyzer to assist either you or an on-board computer in making the necessary adjustments. But because our hearing takes account of the direct, first-arrival sound from the loudspeakers as well as the integrated room response, such compensation is seldom as effective as one might hope, especially at middle and high frequencies. Often it makes the sound worse. Instead, you're usually better off taking an equalizer literally as a much expanded set of tone controls that can be used to fix up the frequency balance of poorly made recordings or even of your loudspeakers.

Although an equalizer can be placed between a preamp and power amp, the best location usually is a tape-monitor loop, where you can switch it in and out of the circuit easily. Nearly all equalizers include a tape-monitor loop to replace the one they take up. Some also enable you to switch the equalizer circuits into the signal path to an attached tape deck so that you can make equalized recordings.

Surround-Sound Processors

As we discussed in Chapter 2, surround-sound is now an important part of a complete audio-video system. One important reason is that the Dolby Surround information encoded in the soundtracks of many movies is carried over onto the soundtracks of their laser videodisc and hi-fi videocassette releases. (And some television programs are now being broadcast in Dolby Surround on an experimental basis.) Even a relatively simple and inexpensive decoder can extract the surround channel and route it to one or more speakers in the back of the room with gratifying results. The Dolby Surround decoders built into some audio-video receivers are mostly of this type.

Superior results can be obtained by using a Pro Logic Dolby Surround processor, whose circuits closely mimic those of theater decoders. Pro Logic adds what is known as *logic steering* to enhance separation between the main and surround channels and to lock mono information into a dedicated center channel, mostly to prevent dialogue from wandering. The performance of Pro Logic decoders is significantly and obviously superior to that of basic Dolby Surround processors, greatly enhancing the realism of the presentation. Although Pro Logic is gradually finding its way into audio-video receivers and amplifiers, most such processors are stand-alone units that go between preamp and power amps or patch into a tape-monitor loop.

All Pro Logic decoders provide at least four outputs: main left and right, center, and surround. Usually there are two rear outputs, even though there is only one surround channel, because the surround effect tends to work better when the sound is diffused by coming from multiple sources. Some have a subwoofer output, and most include a "phantom center" feature that splits the dialogue-channel information equally between the left and right main speakers (useful if you find adding a center speaker impractical). The surround-channel signal undergoes the most processing, passing through a Dolby B noise-

A Surround-Sound Processor. Most are designed primarily for decoding Dolby Surround soundtracks on laser videodiscs, hi-fi videocassettes, and even some stereo TV broadcasts; some are intended mainly for enhancement of music recordings by means of ambience synthesis; and a handful are adept at both.

reduction circuit, a filter that rolls off response below 100 Hz and above 7 kHz (per Dolby Surround specifications), and a 20- to 30-millisecond delay line.

In a Dolby theater presentation, the main speaker really is the one for the center channel, which means that it shoulders quite a heavy burden. In an ideal home Dolby Surround setup, the center speaker would be the same model as that used for the main stereo pair, to prevent distracting alterations in the character of sounds that pan across the screen. (Even though the surround loudspeakers are the least critical, it still is best to use models that sound similar to the front speakers.) But this ideal is often impractical. To accommodate situations in which the center channel must go to a compact loudspeaker or the small speakers built into a monitor, some processors enable you to divide center-channel signals below about 100 Hz between the main stereo speakers, preventing loss of bass and minimizing the chance that the center speaker might be driven into distortion. (This works best if the crossover is steeper than a simple 6-dB-per-octave filter.)

If you have never heard a Dolby Pro Logic Surround system in operation, you owe it to yourself to seek out a demonstration. It can literally transform your experience of home video. Much the same can be said of another type of surround-sound, devoted to enhancing the realism of music reproduction. The last few years have seen the introduction of highly sophisticated ambience-recovery devices based on digital signal processing (DSP). These concert-hall simulators re-create in your living room a pattern of acoustic reflections similar to those in a real performing space. Most provide a number of preprogrammed settings, often based on the characteristics of real places, ranging from a small club to a cathedral or stadium. Usually you can modify these to suit your taste and even store the changes for future recall.

Like Dolby Surround decoders, ambience synthesizers require extra loudspeakers—at least one pair at the rear or sides of the room and possibly another pair at the front in addition to the main stereo speakers. And again, the effect will be best if they share a similar tonal quality.

The number of DSP-based ambience-synthesis systems is small but growing. Curiously, few of them make more than rudimentary provision for Dolby Surround decoding (some none at all), although this seems to be changing. Dolby Surround processors, on the other hand, almost always have some settings designed for music, but the results typically are rather primitive compared to what a good DSP ambience synthesizer can do.

Headphones

For private listening, whether to avoid disturbing others or to shut out the noisy world around you, headphones are the answer. Most familiar nowadays are the small, lightweight models that come with portable cassette players, but there are other types as well. Regardless of size or shape, however, nearly all use a single dynamic or planar-magnetic driver for each ear (a few high-end models have electrostatic drivers).

One of the most obvious and important differences between headphones is the way in which the drivers are housed. The first stereo headphones used what are known as *circumaural earcups,* which fit completely over the outer ear and seal against the side of the head. This design helps improve bass response and can do a good job of isolating the listener from outside sounds. Some people find them uncomfortable, however, and you may prefer not to lose all contact with the sounds going on around you.

Much more popular now are headsets whose earpieces rest lightly against the outside of the ear. These provide less isolation and usually poorer deep-bass response, but most people find them much more comfortable to wear for extended periods. It was from these on-the-ear designs that the miniature headphones sold with personal cassette players evolved. Headphones intended primarily for home use usually have full-size phone plugs, whereas the ones built for portable listening normally have the smaller mini plugs. Fortunately, adapters are available to mate either type of plug with the opposite type of jack.

Choosing headphones is an even more subjective process than selecting speakers. The only really useful specifications you're likely to find are for weight and cord length. Probably the best strategy is to find some candidates that feel comfortable to you. (That way you

Headphones. This is a circumaural design (one that covers the ears and seals against the head). Note the miniplug at the end of the cord and the phone-plug adapter so that you can use the headset with the jacks on home components.

won't waste a lot of time listening to headsets that you would hate wearing no matter how good they sounded.) Then listen to a variety of familiar music on each of the finalists. As with loudspeakers, you're looking for a smooth, natural tonal balance with enough response in the high treble and low bass to give the music sparkle and body. Remember that any sort of peakiness or roughness in the sound will be even more annoying on headphones than it would be on speakers.

Cable

Choosing cables to hook your equipment together used to be one of the easiest parts of buying an audio system (if you had to choose at all). Now it is arguably one of the most confusing. Today you confront a bewildering variety of cables boasting all sorts of exotic materials and construction techniques, for which their makers claim astonishing virtues. Can you really hear wire? If so, what makes one kind better than another?

The most basic electrical characteristic of a wire is its impedance, which has three components: *resistance, capacitance,* and *inductance.* Resistance, measured in ohms, impedes the flow of an electrical current equally at all frequencies. Inductance, which is expressed in henries or millihenries (mH), is similar except that its effect increases with frequency. Capacitance, rated in farads, microfarads (μF), or picofarads (pF), goes the other way, attenuating low frequencies more than high. The interaction of these types of impedance can yield other results—a series resistance in parallel with a capacitance rolls off high frequencies, for example—but until recently, no one claimed that they could not, taken together, adequately describe the electrical characteristics of an audio cable.

In speaker cable, what usually is most important is the resistance, which should be as low as possible to minimize power loss. This also helps keep the impedance of the source (amplifier output impedance plus cable impedance) low, relative to that of the speaker. If the ratio of these impedances, called the *damping factor,* becomes too low, it may cause small frequency-response errors.

Resistance for a given length of cable decreases as the diameter of the wire is increased, so the greater the distance between your amplifier and your speakers, the thicker the cable should be. For runs up to about twenty feet, 16- or even 18-gauge copper wire usually is good enough, easy to handle, and available at low cost from just about any hardware store or electronics retailer. Avoid thinner wire (larger gauge numbers) and aluminum, which is a significantly poorer conductor than copper. If you must use very long cables, move up to 14- or 12-gauge wire. One advantage of some of the thick specialty cables is their use of many fine strands, carefully wound to maintain flexibility;

heavy gauges of ordinary zip cord tend to be stiff and difficult to manage.

Cables conveying line-level signals between electronic components (CD player and receiver, for example) don't have to carry large currents, making resistance less of an issue. For unusually long runs, it is a good idea to make sure the cable is a low-capacitance variety, to prevent any loss of high frequencies within the audio band. This is a very uncommon problem, however.

A more likely source of difficulty is interference picked up by a cable and fed into an amplifier along with the audio signal, creating noise. For this reason, all line-level audio cables have a shield around the conductor, which is grounded through the outer portion, or *skirt,* of an RCA-type pin connector. The best shields are foil, but they also are relatively stiff and easily damaged. More popular are braided-copper shields, which work very well if they are dense enough. Probably the most important differences between interconnect cables are in the quality of their shields, the sturdiness of their plugs, and the security of the connections between the plugs and the conductor and the shield.

Gold-plated connectors are popular on high-end components and cables, and they are worthwhile insofar as they prevent corrosion. However, you can get much the same benefit by periodically unplugging and reinserting ordinary connectors, to wipe away any corrosion that may have accumulated at the junction between plug and jack.

The claims made for certain cables go far beyond such ordinary considerations, however, and often are based on theories more relevant to transmission of radio-frequency signals over miles of wire than to audio frequencies traveling only a few feet. Such concepts as *characteristic impedance* and *skin effect,* to take a couple of prominent examples, simply are not applicable to anything that goes on in an audio system. Some cables have been promoted on the basis of their ability to reduce waveform distortions that occur only at frequencies of several megahertz, far, far above the range of human hearing. Other dubious claims have included the idea that an audio signal actually travels through the insulating portion of a cable, rather than through the conductor, and that wires should be as skinny as possible to minimize random motion of electrons (promulgated by someone with a very poor grasp of the size of subatomic particles).

Cables that meet the traditional standards outlined above will sound identical simply because they will not audibly change the signals passing through them. This does not mean that you should take the cables in your system for granted. Make certain they are well made and, in the case of speaker cable especially, adequate to the task. But for the most part, the cables packed in the boxes with whatever components you buy will do just fine.

Signal-Processor Specifications

Frequency Response
Equalizers, surround-sound decoders, and other signal-processing devices should have flat response within a small fraction of a decibel over the audio band (certainly no worse than $\pm\frac{1}{2}$ dB from 20 Hz to 20 kHz) when their processing circuits are defeated or set to neutral. When they are active, most alter the frequency response purposely to achieve their effects.

Signal-to-Noise (S/N) Ratio
Expect equalizers to have signal-to-noise ratios of 90 dB or better. The S/N of a surround-sound processor usually varies according to the mode it's in and the channel that you measure (effects channels typically being noisier than the main stereo channels). Usually it should be 80 dB or more in the main channels and better than 60 dB in the surround channels.

Distortion
Distortion should be less than 0.1 percent in the main stereo channels. By their nature, surround-sound processors may generate considerably greater distortion than that in their surround channels (several percent), but this is not normally cause for concern.

Headphone Specifications

Try them on and listen. The specifications (if any) won't help much.

Cable Specifications

Capacitance
Audio interconnect cables typically have a capacitance of about 30 picofarads (pF) per foot, which is fine for most applications. Only in very long runs or in tonearm leads is the cable capacitance critical.

Gauge
For speaker wire, the most important characteristics besides the material (which should be copper) are length and thickness, because these determine the cable's resistance. The thicker the wire, the lower its resistance for any given length—and the lower its gauge number. For runs of 20 feet or less, 16-gauge lamp cord certainly is adequate and 18-gauge usually will do. Avoid the skinny (22-gauge or less) cables sometimes passed off as "speaker wire."

Chapter 11

The Future

The Future

Probably all of us have, at one time or another, been struck by the fear that what we buy today may be obsolete tomorrow, or at least that something better will be available. Should I buy a CD player now when recordable CDs or DAT (digital audio tape) may come out next year? Should I buy a new monitor when people are saying HDTV (high-definition television) is "just around the corner?" This peculiar byproduct of rapid technological change can lead to a state of paralysis in which you never stop waiting for the better equipment soon to come. With that in mind, we've assembled a brief guide to the major new audio and video technologies known to be waiting in the wings.

DAT: Digital Audio Tape

After several years of political battling between the record industry and manufacturers of audio equipment, it now appears that DAT decks will be officially introduced sometime in mid-1990. The machines offered then will differ in one important respect from the decks now available in Japan and, in very limited quantities, here: They will enable you to make direct digital copies of CDs and prerecorded DATs, which means there will be no loss of quality. (You will not, however, be able to make direct digital dubs of the resulting tape copies.) Currently, only professional machines can do that.

DAT has several significant advantages over the familiar analog cassette system. The tapes are smaller, for one thing—almost *too* small—and hold as much as two hours of uninterrupted music. Because the recordings are digital, there is no need for noise reduction or fussy tape-matching adjustments. Digital subcodes on the tape permit high-speed searches to any point in a recording. And sound quality is equal to that of Compact Discs, with sixteen-bit encoding at a sampling rate of 44.1 kHz or 48 kHz.

The main disadvantage of DAT is cost: Even the cheapest DAT deck will always be more expensive than a low-end cassette deck or CD player. A DAT recorder has to include both analog-to-digital (A/D) and digital-to-analog (D/A) converters, and the tape transport is like a miniaturized VCR mechanism that uses tiny heads on a rapidly spinning drum to pack huge amounts of digital data onto the narrow, slow-moving tape. The DAT cassettes themselves are more costly than analog cassettes because they must be molded more precisely and contain hard-to-make metal-evaporated tape, which is needed to support the extremely high data density.

Although DAT does appear to be on the verge of widespread availability, it is not going to supplant the Compact Disc. CDs are

A DAT Cassette

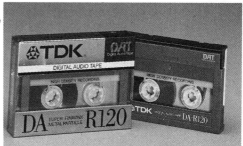

both cheaper and more durable, and you can jump between selections almost instantly on a disc—a capability DAT can't match even with its high-speed search capability. The Compact Disc will remain the preferred medium for high-quality prerecorded music for many years to come.

DAT has a much better shot at displacing high-end analog cassette decks. The higher quality of DAT recordings, the superior convenience features of DAT decks, and the ability to create direct digital copies of CDs will make the new format the preferred choice of home recordists who want the very best. Nonetheless, it is unlikely that DAT will supplant the analog cassette entirely. The cassette format is capable of very good performance, and it is both cheap and deeply entrenched; it's the most popular medium for recorded music in history. It has been estimated that there are at least three cassette mechanisms in the United States for every man, woman, and child.

Dolby S

Enter the latest from Dolby Labs: S-type noise reduction. Derived from the very sophisticated professional SR system introduced a few years ago, Dolby S promises noise reduction over the full audio band, with a maximum improvement of approximately 24 decibels at high frequencies—more than double what you get from Dolby B. Moreover, Dolby claims that S-type noise reduction sounds better undecoded than previous schemes and is less finicky about things like frequency-response errors than is Dolby C. Even so, Dolby will place more stringent performance requirements on its licensees for decks that incorporate the S system.

The result will be a new generation of analog cassette decks capable of making better recordings than ever before, arriving probably at about the same time as DAT. Dolby S will not make analog cassettes sound better than DAT, or even as good, but it will bring them a step closer. And cassettes recorded with Dolby S should play back passably well in your current decks equipped with Dolby B. That, in turn, will be an incentive for record companies to release prerecorded cassettes with Dolby S encoding. Although the almost certain success of S-type noise reduction does not imply failure for DAT, it provides an interesting alternative, which probably will slow the growth of the digital competition.

Recordable Compact Discs

Somewhat more distant than either of the above developments is the prospect for CDs that can be used much the way we use tape now: recorded, played back, erased, and recorded again. Such *CD-Rs,* as they are often called, are in development, however, and some have estimated that the discs and machines to record them could be available at reasonable prices by late 1990. Given the time needed to arrive at standards and the political squabbling that seems to attend the introduction of digital recording systems, that is probably optimistic. But it does seem likely that recordable CD will emerge from the laboratory sometime in the next few years.

How CD-R will fare when it finally arrives is far from clear. If DAT is at all successful, CD-R will face an established digital recording medium that boasts smaller size and longer playing time. CD-R, on the other hand, should be a more rugged medium and will share with regular Compact Discs the benefit of extremely quick access to any point in a recording. It may also be cheaper than DAT.

In short, the entire future of home digital recording is up in the air right now and seems unlikely to be resolved until the mid-1990s.

All-Digital Audio Systems

The Compact Disc brought with it a tantalizing vision: audio systems that keep signals in digital form all the way to the power amplifier, converting them to analog only at the point where it becomes absolutely necessary. This would eliminate the need for D/A converters in every digital component, reduce opportunities for addition of noise and distortion, and make possible all sorts of fancy digital signal processing. Because digital signal processing (DSP) is done arithmetically—adding, subtracting, multiplying, and dividing numbers—it can be extraordinarily flexible and powerful. Currently, the most visible application of DSP is in ambience synthesizers, but digital equalizers, compressors, expanders, and so forth are also possible.

The downside of a digital control center is that all analog inputs, such as those from tuners, turntables, and regular cassette decks, must be converted to digital and then back to analog. And at least for now, analog processing is less costly than digital. Consequently, the "all-digital" system is going to be slow in coming, although one can see inklings of it in a few products (including one genuine digital preamplifier) and in the growing number of amplifiers that have digital inputs and D/A converters for CD players.

Fortunately, most of what you need in the way of signal processing can be done adequately, if not spectacularly, by analog means, and there are add-on DSP processors for the rest. In other words, digital systems are definitely something to look forward to, but they are not something you should feel the need to wait for.

Digital Video

Video can benefit at least as much as audio from digital recording methods, and work is well underway on that front. Digital video recorders are already available to professionals, though at staggering cost. Just as happened with analog video recording, we can expect the technology to trickle down eventually into products for the home. The result will be a great leap forward in the quality of taped images.

This is a good ways off, however. Don't postpone buying an S-VHS or Hi8 VCR in anticipation of digital VCRs tomorrow. You'll have a long wait.

HDTV: High-Definition Television

HDTV is one of those things that seem always to be just a few years away. When it does arrive, high-definition television will approximately double the resolution of the pictures we receive and widen them to approximate the aspect ratio of most feature films (about five units of width for every three of height, as opposed to the 4:3 ratio of current television systems). And the sound probably will be of CD quality, transmitted digitally. HDTV still won't look as good as a well-projected 35mm motion picture, but it will be much closer than what you get on your screen today.

Periodically, HDTV gets a lot of attention in the press, leading people to expect that it is just around the corner. In fact, it is mired in a tangle of technical and regulatory issues that will take years to resolve. For the United States, HDTV almost certainly will not arrive in commercial form until the mid-1990s, and the turn of the century is probably a more realistic target, assuming that it makes it at all. If and

The Wide-Screen Advantage. Perhaps the greatest benefit of HDTV will be the wider aspect ratio it will bring to the screen—essentially the same as that for standard theater projection. This will give television pictures a much more natural and pleasing look and greatly reduce the problems now associated with preparing movies for broadcast and release on disc and tape.

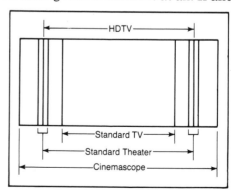

when HDTV does get here, the receivers will be very costly.

As with digital video recording, this is not a case where you should put off the pleasures available now in anticipation of those that may become available later. If you want a better monitor, go ahead and get one.

IDTV: Improved-Definition Television

At that point, however, you may find yourself confronting another set of initials and wondering what to do. Unlike HDTV, IDTV (improved-definition television) is not a wholesale revamping of the TV broadcast system. All the changes are in the receiver and are de-signed to extract more vertical detail from ordinary NTSC video sig-nals by doubling the number of scanning lines displayed in each pass of the electron guns across the face of the screen. Every company that makes IDTV monitors does it a little differently from the others, and most incorporate some other features, such as video noise reduction, but always at the core is detail enhancement.

The basic technique is known as *noninterlaced scanning.* Usually it is achieved by digitizing the video signal as it comes in and storing it in a memory capable of holding one full 262.5-line field, so that infor-mation from successive fields can be used to build a complete 525-line frame every sixtieth of a second instead of every thirtieth. If nothing in the image is moving, the monitor can simply display two fields si-multaneously, but this is a rare situation. When there is motion (which is most of the time), the monitor must think a little harder in order to avoid smearing the image, since the fields are scanned a sixti-eth of a second apart at the camera. For example, in some areas of the screen it may have to interpolate between the lines of a field to get ap-propriate information. The application of this and other strategies for dealing with the complexities of noninterlaced scanning is known as *motion compensation.*

Motion compensation is the hard part of IDTV, and, if it is not done very well, reproduction will be noticeably inferior to that of a good standard monitor. (Unfortunately, the sets that stand to benefit most from good IDTV, those with large screens, also are the ones that show up the inadequacies of poor designs most readily.) Most current IDTV sets produce at least some annoying artifacts, so look carefully before you buy. Watch for smearing or *jaggies* (a stepped or slightly blocky quality on moving objects in an image). These are telltale signs of inadequate motion compensation.

Some IDTV monitors do not have these problems, and the tech-nology will improve over time. Even so, make your decisions based on actual performance, not on the presence or absence of a feature that is supposed to make it better. The best monitors in the world still are the professional displays (typically priced at about $8,000 for a 19-inch set without a tuner), none of which use IDTV techniques.

Appendix

Answers to Common Questions

Answers to Common Questions

Many of the subjects discussed below are covered or at least touched upon earlier in the book. However, we feel that the following specific questions come up often enough to deserve special attention.

Q. *Where is the best place to buy equipment?*

A. For most people, it's a store that offers good service, a reasonably wide selection of high-quality brands, and a good listening and viewing environment. Look for salespeople who are knowledgeable about the products they are selling and who will take the time to explain and demonstrate them properly. A good dealer will listen to your needs and not try to pressure you into a hasty or uncomfortable decision. A store that meets these criteria probably will not offer the very lowest prices you can find, but you stand a much better chance of walking out the door with a system that will give you long-term satisfaction.

Also, beware of dealers selling merchandise intended for other markets and brought here through channels other than the manufacturer's official U.S. distribution network. Such "gray-market" goods often carry a lower price than similar products at authorized dealers, but their warranties may not be valid in this country.

Q. *How should I allocate my money when buying a system?*

A. This question gets harder all the time, as the number of options available multiplies. For a basic audio system in the $600–$1,000 range, it usually is best to split your money evenly among three or, at most, four components. As you move up the price ladder, let the speakers take a larger proportion of the total budget. The proper division of resources for an audio-video or surround-sound system depends so much on your individual requirements that a blanket recommendation is impossible. A good dealer will help guide you to a balanced system. One other important point to remember: When shopping, think about the future as well as the present. Especially if you're on a tight budget, try to choose a few good pieces that can serve as the foundation for a more complete system down the road.

Q. *I've hooked up everything, but I'm not getting any sound (or picture). What should I do?*

A. Start with the obvious. Is everything electronic plugged in? Are all the components interconnected properly? Are their controls set correctly? For example, engaging the tape/monitor switch will kill the sound if no tape is playing. (If you haven't looked at the manuals for your equipment, do so now!) Assuming that everything is installed correctly, the next step is to isolate the problem. Check to see if it occurs on all sources (CD, tuner, tape, and so forth) or on only one. If the problem occurs with all sources, it probably resides with your speakers or, more likely, your receiver. If it happens with only one source, that component is the probable culprit. Also try switching cables; you may just have a bad connection.

Q. *How can I improve my FM or television reception?*

A. In most cases, the answer is to get a better antenna, one that is more directional and has higher gain. This will enable you to discriminate against interference by aiming the antenna toward the desired signal and to strengthen weak signals. However, you may still have difficulty getting good reception even of some nearby stations, especially if you live in a city with tall buildings or in an area with a lot of hills. In such locations, *multipath*—which causes distortion on FM and ghosts on TV—can be a nearly intractable problem. Cable may be an alternative for you, but signal quality usually will be worse than what you would get from a cleanly received over-the-air transmission.

Q. *What can I do to make my CDs stop skipping?*

A. Try cleaning the offending discs with a soft cloth, wiping radially from the center to the edge; if necessary, use a little water to remove oily or sticky residues. If the skipping continues, chances are the offending discs are damaged or defective. Or, if you find that you have trouble with many discs, including new ones, your player may need service.

Q. *What kind of tape should I use in my cassette deck?*

A. The kind that gives you the best recordings. That may sound like a flippant answer, but it's true. The relationship between deck and tape is a very intimate one that works best when the two are well matched. Unless your deck gives you some means of adjusting bias and sensitivity, a theoretically superior tape may give worse results than one for which the deck was adjusted at the factory. Some manufacturers give recommendations in their manuals. Otherwise, try some different brands and grades of tape to see which work best for you.

Q. *What's the best location for loudspeakers?*

A. It depends on their design. Most are designed for best performance when placed near or against one wall and several feet from others, either on the floor or on a support that puts the tweeter approximately at ear level. There are plenty of exceptions, however—speakers that work best several feet from any walls and even speakers designed specifically for corner placement, which normally is the least desirable alternative. And you should always experiment because the exact results will depend on the acoustics of the room. Some (though not enough) manufacturers give very specific placement recommendations, which should serve as a good starting point.

Q. *My system seems to pick up radio transmissions, even when I'm not using the tuner. What can I do to get rid of this interference?*

A. Radio-frequency interference, or RFI, is most commonly picked up through the phono inputs of a receiver or amplifier, but that is far from the only path. In some cases, it enters the amplifier through the speaker leads. Standard treatments include cleaning connectors and rerouting cables. Changing the length of a cable or replacing it with one having better shielding sometimes helps. If all else fails, try moving your equipment to a different place in the room; small changes in position sometimes make a big difference.

Q. *What can I do to get rid of hum in my system?*

A. As with RFI, the solution sometimes involves rerouting cables, in this case away from AC line cords. Hum may also occur if your turntable or tape deck is too close to a large power transformer, such as the one in your receiver or amplifier. Severe hum on phono usually is caused by the turntable's ground lead not being connected to the ground terminal on the receiver or amplifier, though in rare cases, hum may actually be reduced by disconnecting it. Mild hum may be reduced slightly by reorienting power-cord plugs in their sockets.

Q. *My system sometimes thumps or pops when I switch sources or turn it on or off. Is this a sign of trouble?*

A. Probably not, unless the noises are very loud. Some receivers and amplifiers just do that.

Q. *Sometimes I hear the sound from one input faintly in the background of another. What's going on?*

A. You're hearing leakage between the inputs, called *crosstalk*. This shouldn't happen in a well-designed component, but unless you can hear the unwanted input over the music on the one you've selected, it's harmless.

Q. *The hi-fi track on some tapes cuts in and out on my VCR. How can I make this stop?*

A. Adjust the tracking control. If that doesn't work, the next-best alternative may be to turn off the hi-fi sound when playing the offending tapes.

Q. *The bass from my speakers is weaker than I had expected. What's wrong?*

A. They may just need to be closer to a wall or the floor. Or they may be wired out of phase. The latter is especially likely if the stereo image seems vague and diffuse. Try reversing the hot and ground (plus and minus) leads at one end of one speaker cable. If the speakers were previously wired out of phase, both the bass and the stereo image will improve.